The Danger of Loving Money

The Danger of Loving Money

by
John MacArthur, Jr.

MOODY PRESS
CHICAGO

ISBN: 0-8024-5380-5

1 2 3 4 5 6 Printing/LC/Year 93 92 91 90 89

Contents

These Bible studies are taken from messages delivered by Pastor-Teacher John MacArthur, Jr., at Grace Community Church in Panorama City, California. The recorded messages themselves may be purchased as a series or individually. Please request the current price list by writing to:

The Master's Communication
P.O. Box 4000
Panorama City, CA 91412

Or call the following toll-free number:
1-800-55-GRACE

1
The Danger of Loving Money

Outline

Introduction
A. The Theme
  1. The right attitude about money
  2. The wrong affection for money
B. The Transition

Lesson
I. The Principle (vv. 6-9)
  A. The Nature of Loving Money (vv. 6-8)
    1. It ignores true gain (v. 6)
      a) The elements of true riches
        (1) Godliness
        (2) Contentment
          (a) Its use in classical Greek
          (b) Its use by Paul
      b) The desire for many riches
        (1) Those who desire least
        (2) Those who desire most
          (a) Secular examples
          (b) Biblical exhortations
    2. It focuses on the temporal (v. 7)
      a) The reality of man's life
      b) The reality of money's value
    3. It obscures the simplicity of life (v. 8)
      a) Losing the simple joys in life
      b) Recovering the simple joys in life
  B. The Effect of Loving Money (v. 9)
    1. It leads to sinful entrapment (v. 9a)
    2. It makes us succumb to harmful desires (v. 9b)

3. It results in eternal damnation (9c)
   a) Defining the terms
      (1) Drown
      (2) Destruction
      (3) Perdition
   b) Examining the Scriptures
II. The Proof (v. 10)
   A. Their Departing from the Truth
   B. Their Suffering Many Sorrows

Conclusion

Introduction

A. The Theme

First Timothy 6:10 says, "The love of money is the root of all evil." That is the focal point of verses 6-10. Everything before and after that statement is an exposition of its significance. Scripture is replete with injunctions against loving money. Perhaps the most important is this one from our Lord: "Where your treasure is, there will your heart be also" (Matt. 6:21). What we do with our money reveals the priorities of our hearts.

1. The right attitude about money

What should our attitude be toward money? Scripture has much to say on the subject.

a) We are not to view money as wrong in itself

In Proverbs 8:21 God says to those who love wisdom, "I will fill their treasuries." The Bible doesn't say it is wrong to have money.

b) We are not to assume we acquire money on our own

Deuteronomy 8:18 says that God "giveth thee power to get wealth." We don't earn anything apart from the providence of God.

c) We are not to cling to money against God's will

God may choose to take money away from us. That happened to Job (1:14-19) and to the apostles, who said to Jesus, "We have forsaken all, and followed thee" (Matt. 19:27). We are not to hold onto money if God wants us to let go of it.

d) We are not to show favoritism to those who have money

James 2:1-10 warns against favoring the rich over the poor. We ought to have more concern for the poor because their needs are so great.

e) We are not to be proud of our money

First Timothy 6:17 says, "Charge them that are rich in this age, that they be not high-minded." We should not be conceited about all that we possess.

f) We are not to seek riches

We are to seek first the kingdom of God and allow Him to meet our needs (Matt. 6:33).

g) We are not to substitute money for trust in God

First Timothy 6:17 also says that the rich are not to "trust in uncertain riches but in the living God."

h) We are not to hoard money selfishly

Proverbs 11:25 says, "The liberal soul shall be made fat, and he that watereth shall be watered also himself." In Luke 6:38 Jesus says, "Give, and it shall be given unto you." Sacrificial generosity should be a mark of every believer.

i) We are not to love money

This is the overarching principle regarding money: "For the love of money is the root of all evil" (1 Tim. 6:10).

2. The wrong affection for money

The love of money is the root of all kinds of evil. The Greek word translated "love of money" (*philarguria*) means "affection for silver." Paul is discussing an attitude about money, not money itself. There is nothing inherently wrong with money.

Paul is talking about the sin of greed. He says that the love of money is the "root"—the source of all kinds of evil. Usually if you love money, nothing can stop your pursuit of it. Therefore, that obsession leads to all kinds of sin. However, if you are consumed with loving the Lord your God with all your heart, soul, mind, and strength, you will set aside anything that may hinder your pursuit of Him. That's why you cannot love and serve both God and money (Matt. 6:24).

How to Know If You Love Money

1. You spend more time thinking about how to get money than on how to pursue excellence in your work.

   Are you more concerned with how much you make or the quality of your service? Is your job a means to finance your indulgences, or a means by which you can glorify God? Our response to daily tasks reveals much about whether we love money or not.

2. You never seem to have enough.

   A person who loves money is never satisfied with what he has. He hasn't learned to be content in whatever state he finds himself (Phil. 4:11).

3. You flaunt what you own.

   People who love money derive an inordinate amount of pleasure from wearing, driving, living in, and showing off what they buy.

4. You resent giving it to others.

   It pains people to give even to a worthy cause when they're preoccupied with self-gratification. The idea of giving or sharing is distasteful to them.

5. You sin to obtain money.

   Some people will lie on their income tax returns, cheat on their expense accounts, steal from the till at their jobs, or compromise their convictions to obtain money. Any time you sin to get money, you prove that you love money more than you love God and His righteousness.

If any of those statements reflect your actions and attitudes regarding money, be warned that such love for money will produce all kinds of evil in your life (1 Tim. 6:10). If you continue, you are succumbing to the deceitfulness of riches (Matt. 13:22).

Loving Money vs. Having Money

Some can have a lot of money and not love it, whereas others can have next to no money and love what little they have. I know people who have a tremendous amount of money, yet do not love it. In fact, they spend their lives doing their best to glorify God. They aren't consumed with pursuing money; they're consumed with pursuing God. They don't flaunt their money or the things they possess. They don't sin or compromise to get money. But for His own reasons, God has determined to give them much.

At the same time, I have met people who have no money yet are desperately in love with it. They spend most of their time figuring out how to get more of it. The danger of loving money is not dependent on how much you have.

B. The Transition

   Who prompted Paul to discuss the love of money? The false teachers who were faking godliness and were motivated by the potential for material gain (1 Tim. 6:5). In verse 6 he counters, "But godliness with contentment is great gain." The false teacher who supposes that his pretensions of godliness will bring him great gain is wrong—only true godliness results in great gain. Beginning in verse 6 Paul talks about money in a general sense, and he ends in verse 10 by warning us about the danger of loving money. Though Paul's discussion was aimed at those in the Ephesian church who were abusing money, it has great relevance for us today.

Lesson

I. THE PRINCIPLE (vv. 6-9)

Loving money results in all kinds of evil. That means that loving it is very hazardous.

A. The Nature of Loving Money (vv. 6-8)

1. It ignores true gain (v. 6)

   "But godliness with contentment is great gain."

   The Greek word translated "but" (*de*) can also be translated "indeed." By using "indeed" we would understand Paul to be following verse 5 with the statement, "Indeed godliness with contentment is great gain." If we use "but" we would understand Paul to be speaking in an adversative sense: "But as opposed to false godliness that doesn't provide any gain, true godliness does provide gain." The way we translate it doesn't change the fact that there is great gain in true godliness.

   a) The elements of true riches

   (1) Godliness

   "Godliness" (Gk., *eusebeia*) is often used in the pastoral epistles. It means "reverence" or "piety." I like to think of it as God-likeness. There is great gain in reflecting God's nature and being content with the way things are in your life. But if all you want is money, you'll never have great gain because you'll never be content. A contented godliness produces a gain that money can't buy— a spiritual gain.

(2) Contentment

Genuine "great gain" comes from true godliness, which is inseparably linked to contentment. The Greek word translated contentment (*autarkēs*) means "self-sufficiency."

(*a*) Its use in classical Greek

The Cynics and Stoics used the word *autarkēs* to refer to self-mastery. To them a contented person had inner resources that allowed him to be unflappable in the face of external distractions. Even when he was not able to control his circumstances, he could control his reactions to them. *Autarkēs* basically means "to be sufficient," "to seek nothing more," "to be content with what you have."

(*b*) Its use by Paul

Though *autarkēs* is a noble human trait, Paul stretched its meaning further.

(i) 2 Corinthians 3:5—"Not that we are sufficient of ourselves to think anything as of ourselves, but our sufficiency is of God."

(ii) 2 Corinthians 9:8—"God is able to make all grace abound toward you, that ye, always having all sufficiency in all things, may abound to every good work."

(iii) Philippians 4:11-13, 19—"I have learned to be content whatever the circumstances. I know what it is to be in need, and I know what it is to have plenty. I have learned the secret of being content in any and every situation, whether well fed or hungry, whether living in plenty

13

or in want. I can do everything through him who gives me strength. . . . My God will meet all your needs according to his glorious riches in Christ Jesus" (NIV*).

Paul elevated the meaning of *autarkēs* by using it to refer to the sufficiency of God, not man. Christian contentment is more than self-mastery or human virtue. It is intrinsically related to the sufficiency of God and Christ. A truly contented person wants to live within God's sovereign, providential will and seeks to be like Him.

b) The desire for many riches

True godliness brings about true gain because it produces contentment. The person who is rich in the biblical sense doesn't need anything more.

(1) Those who desire least

The Epicureans believed that the secret to contentment was not to add to a man's possessions, but to take away his desires. Paul echoed that sentiment in Philippians 4:11-13.

(*a*) Proverbs 30:8-9—"Give me neither poverty nor riches; feed me with food convenient for me, lest I be full, and deny thee, and say, Who is the Lord? Or lest I be poor, and steal, and take the name of my God in vain." The writer of that proverb didn't want too much or too little; he was content with whatever God planned to provide him. True godliness is great gain. The *gain* in this instance is not related to how much you have, but to how much you want. If you are content with what God has given you, you are rich.

(*b*) Hebrews 13:5—"Let your manner of life be without covetousness, and be content with

* New International Version.

such things as ye have; for he hath said, I will never leave thee, nor forsake thee." What more could anyone want than to know God and to receive what He has given?

If you spend your life chasing after money, you'll forfeit true gain because you'll never get enough to satisfy yourself. A godly person is motivated not by the love of money but by the love of God. He seeks the greatest riches: spiritual contentment and complete faith in the omnipresent and omnipotent God.

(2) Those who desire most

(a) Secular examples

It has been well-documented that some wealthy men obsessed with money, such as John Jacob Astor and Cornelius Vanderbilt, are extremely miserable. Some rich men, such as Henry Ford, develop an aversion to wealth, yearning for the simpler days. Although ungodly men never understand this fact, only those who experience the spiritual contentment that comes through godliness are truly rich.

(b) Biblical exhortations

(i) Psalm 63:1-5—"O God, thou art my God, early will I seek thee; my soul thirsteth for thee, my flesh longeth for thee in a dry and thirsty land, where no water is, to see thy power and thy glory, as I have seen thee in the sanctuary. Because thy lovingkindness is better than life, my lips shall praise thee. Thus will I bless thee while I live; I will lift up my hands in thy name. My soul shall be satisfied." David was satisfied in his communion with the eternal God; he loved and was loved by Him.

15

(ii) Psalm 107:9—"He satisfieth the longing soul, and filleth the hungry soul with goodness."

(iii) Isaiah 55:2—God said, "Why do ye spend money for that which is not bread? And your labor for that which satisfieth not? Hearken diligently unto me, and eat that which is good, and let your soul delight itself in fatness."

No one will ever be truly satisfied by the pursuit of money, because contentment and the love of money are mutually exclusive. It has been well said that money is like sea water—the more you drink, the thirstier you get.

2. The love of money focuses on the temporal (v. 7)

"We brought nothing into this world, and it is certain we can carry nothing out."

a) The reality of man's life

Every baby is born stark naked. We bring nothing into this world, and we take nothing out of it.

(1) Job 1:21—Job said, "Naked came I out of my mother's womb, and naked shall I return."

(2) Ecclesiastes 5:15—"As he came forth of his mother's womb, naked shall he return to go as he came, and shall take nothing of his labor, which he may carry away in his hand."

b) The reality of money's value

If you spend your life loving money, you are pursuing something that has no eternal value.

(1) Matthew 6:19-21—Jesus said, "Lay not up for yourselves treasures upon earth, where moth and rust doth corrupt, and where thieves break through and steal, but lay up for yourselves treasures in heaven, where neither moth nor rust

16

doth corrupt, and where thieves do not break through nor steal; for where your treasure is, there will your heart be also."

(2) Mark 8:36-37—Jesus said, "What shall it profit a man, if he shall gain the whole world, and lose his own soul? Or what shall a man give in exchange for his soul?" If you gained every material possession in the world, you would discover that you had gained nothing—especially if you weren't prepared for eternity when you finally faced death.

People who pursue money as a supreme goal in life focus on the temporal and ignore the eternal.

3. The love of money obscures the simplicity of life (v. 8)

"Having food and raiment let us be therewith content."

The Greek word translated "raiment" refers primarily to clothing but can also include the idea of shelter. Paul is saying that we ought to be content with having food, clothing, and shelter—the basic necessities of life. He doesn't condemn our having more if God graciously chooses to give more. But he does condemn an attitude of discontent.

a) Losing the simple joys in life

Because it is so wealthy, our society tends to replace people with things and conversation with entertainment. We miss out on the simple joys in life. I think most of us long for a life less cluttered by the world's distractions.

The focus of the Christian life should be relationships. However, our relationship to God and our relationships with family and friends are often obscured by our desire to obtain what we do not have. Instead of enjoying life, we're strapped into trying to figure out how we can stretch our paychecks to pay for things we don't even need to buy in the first place. That pressure causes depression because we

17

allow ourselves to go into debt in order to gain those possessions.

b) Recovering the simple joys in life

Jesus clearly stated what the Christian's attitude should be: "Ye cannot serve God and money. Therefore, I say unto you, Be not anxious for your life, what ye shall eat, or what ye shall drink; nor yet for your body, what ye shall put on" (Matt. 6:24-25). In verses 26-31 Jesus describes how God cares for the birds and the lilies of the field. Then He says, "Your heavenly Father knoweth that ye have need of all these things. But seek ye first the kingdom of God, and his righteousness, and all these things shall be added unto you" (vv. 32-33). If we reach the point where we invest all our energy and resources in God's priorities, we will have that simple joy. The simplicity of life is found in accepting what God gives us and refusing to be covetous. When we seek God and His glory and are not consumed with the frivolities of life, nothing can steal our joy.

How to Be Content

How can you be content with the simple things of life and learn not to desire more possessions? Let me give you some principles I have tried to apply in my own life.

1. Acknowledge that the Lord owns everything you have

Before you buy something, ask yourself, *Will this bring glory to God? Will this help to advance His kingdom? Will this make my ministry more effective? Can I use this to show love to others?* Knowing that God is the owner of everything I possess helps me in that decision-making process.

2. Cultivate a thankful heart

When you are thankful for what you have, you are informing God that you are satisfied with what He has given you.

18

3. Discern your needs from your wants

Before you go to the store, ask yourself, *What do I really need?* By answering that simple question, you will find yourself exercising greater control over what you purchase. Ultimately, that will make available more resources that the Lord can use to advance His kingdom.

4. Don't buy what you do not need and cannot use

Ask yourself, *How will this enhance my ability to serve God?* You don't want to be distracted from doing what God wants you to do.

5. Spend less than you make

Save what's left for a purpose that God may put on your heart.

6. Give sacrificially to the Lord

Lay up treasure in heaven for the work of the kingdom.

If you apply those principles to your life, you will prevent yourself from being burdened with a love for money.

The joy of life is not in what you have, but in your relationships with those you know and love. People are valuable; money and possessions are not. I think Jesus had people in mind when He said, "If you have not been trustworthy in handling worldly wealth, who will trust you with true riches?" (Luke 16:11, NIV).

B. The Effect of Loving Money (v. 9)

1. Loving money leads to sinful entrapment (v. 9*a*)

"They that will (Gk., *boulomai*) be rich fall into temptation and a snare."

Boulomai indicates that those people have a set, willful desire to be rich. It's not an emotional response; it is carefully thought out. Such greedy people continually fall into temptation. All kinds of sins ensnare them. Sa-

19

tan sets the trap, and he will hold them in it for as long as he possibly can.

Scripture says much about the snares of sin. Deuteronomy 7:25 is one example: "The carved images of their gods shall ye burn with fire; thou shalt not desire the silver or gold that is on them, nor take it unto thee, lest thou be snared therein; for it is an abomination to the Lord thy God." God warns you not to love money because that will trap you in an odious life-style. In a sense you're like a trapped animal—you reach for the bait and are caught.

2. Loving money makes us succumb to harmful desires (v. 9*b*)

"[They fall] into many foolish and hurtful lusts."

People who love money will be controlled by "foolish" desires. They have a burning desire for self-fulfillment and more money. As a result they become victimized by their own lusts. James says of them, "Ye lust, and have not; ye kill, and desire to have, and cannot obtain; ye fight and war, yet ye have not" (4:2).

The Greek word translated "hurtful" (*blaberos*) means "injurious." That is the opposite of happiness. Chasing after money is not the way to be happy; it's a sure way to be trapped in sin and victimized by lust.

3. It results in eternal damnation (9*c*)

"Which drown men in destruction and perdition."

People's evil impulses ultimately lead them to drown in judgment.

a) Defining the terms

(1) *Drown*—The Greek word translated "drown" refers to dragging to the bottom like a sunken ship. It portrays total devastation. Greedy people simply disappear from sight.

(2) *Destruction*—The Greek word translated "destruction" is used in reference to the destruction of the body. It also is used to describe a general sense of destruction (e.g., 1 Thess. 5:3).

(3) *Perdition*—The Greek word translated "perdition" most often refers to the destruction of the soul. It speaks of the place reserved for the false prophet and the beast—the hell of hells designed for those who do not know God (Rev. 17:8).

Paul is saying that people who determine to be rich experience total devastation of body and soul—total judgment and complete, eternal, irreversible loss. The love of money damns people. It plunges them into an ocean of eternal destruction.

b) Examining the Scriptures

(1) Acts 8:20, 23—When Simon the sorcerer revealed his love for money by stating his desire to purchase the power of the Holy Spirit, Peter said, "Thy money perish with thee. . . . I perceive that thou art in the gall of bitterness, and in the bond of iniquity."

(2) James 5:1-5—"Come now, ye rich men, weep and howl for your miseries that shall come upon you. Your riches are corrupted and your garments are moth-eaten. Your gold and silver are rusted, and the rust of them shall be a witness against you, and shall eat your flesh as it were fire. Ye have heaped treasure together for the last days. Behold, the hire of the laborers who have reaped down your fields, which is of you kept back by fraud, crieth; and the cries of them who have reaped are entered into the ears of the Lord of Sabaoth. Ye have lived in pleasure on the earth, and been wanton; ye have nourished your hearts, as in a day of slaughter." That's one example of sin that comes from the love of money: an employer who loves money so much that he cheats his employees to keep more for himself. But such a man will receive severe judgment.

21

(3) Zephaniah 1:18—"Neither their silver nor their gold shall be able to deliver them in the day of the Lord's wrath."

The love of money is very dangerous. It ensnares people by creating in them irrational desires that bring only harm. Ultimately it leads to damnation.

II. THE PROOF (v. 10)

"The love of money is the root of all evil, which, while some coveted after, they have erred from the faith, and pierced themselves through with many sorrows."

Paul now proves that loving money is indeed dangerous. The Greek word translated "coveted after" refers to reaching after a desire, like stretching forth one's hands as far as possible. It speaks of those who passionately pursue money—perhaps like Demas, who "loved this present world" (2 Tim. 4:10).

A. Their Departing from the Truth

Paul said that such people "have erred from the faith." That means they were led away from the body of Christian truth—the "faith which was once delivered unto the saints" (Jude 3). They were exposed to the truth, but they chose money over God. We've already seen that you can't serve God and money (Matt. 6:24). Sadly, those people chose money.

To whom was Paul alluding? One that immediately comes to mind—although he isn't named in the text—is Judas Iscariot. He loved money and turned from the faith. He was one of Jesus' twelve disciples, yet he desired thirty pieces of silver more than the Son of God. That certainly wasn't a rational choice. But as we have discovered, people like Judas follow their foolish desires to their own peril.

B. Their Suffering Many Sorrows

Paul also said that such people had "pierced themselves through with many sorrows." The Greek word translated "pierced" originally was used of running a skewer through an animal to put it on a spit. Those who love money impale their own souls, bringing upon themselves all-consuming grief. They eventually experience a condemning conscience, an unfulfilled heart, and disillusionment with life. Certainly Judas suffered from those things when he hanged himself. That is no way to live—or die.

Conclusion

How then should we live? By pursuing God, not money. David said, "I shall be satisfied, when I awake, with thy likeness" (Ps. 17:15). Anything we possess should be used only to advance God's kingdom. The love of money is deadly. The one who does so ignores true riches, focuses on the temporal, obscures the simple joys of life, falls into sinful entrapment, succumbs to harmful lusts, and ultimately falls into eternal damnation. How much better to love the Lord your God with all your heart, soul, mind, and strength!

Focusing on the Facts

1. What is the right attitude to have about money (see pp. 8-9)?
2. In what way is the love of money the root of all kinds of evil (see p. 10)?
3. How can you know if you love money (see pp. 10-11)?
4. Is the danger of loving money directly related to how much you have? Explain (see p. 11).
5. What motivated Paul to discuss the love of money in 1 Timothy 6:6-10 (see pp. 11-12)?
6. What is necessary before a believer can experience "great gain" (1 Tim. 6:6; see p. 12)?
7. How did the Cynics and Stoics use the Greek word translated "contentment" (*autarkēs*)? How did Paul use it (see pp. 13-14)?
8. Describe a person who is truly rich (see p. 14).
9. What motivates a godly person (see p. 15)?
10. Why aren't people satisfied with the pursuit of money (see p. 16)?
11. What do people bring into the world with them? What do they take out of it (1 Tim. 6:7; see p. 16)?
12. What is the real value of money (see pp. 16-17)?
13. According to 1 Timothy 6:8, what should make us content (see p. 17)?

14. What ought to be the focus of the Christian life (see p. 17)?
15. What attitude should we have so we can hold onto the simple joys in life (Matt. 6:24-33; see p. 18)?
16. How can we be content (see pp. 18-19)?
17. What two things happen to those who desire to be rich? Explain each (1 Tim. 6:9; see pp. 19-20).
18. How does Paul characterize the desires of those who love money? Explain (1 Tim. 6:9; see p. 20).
19. What ultimately happens to those who continue to love money? Explain (1 Tim. 6:9; see pp. 20-21).
20. What two proofs does Paul offer to show that loving money is the root of all kinds of evil? Explain each (1 Tim. 6:10; see pp. 22-23)?

Pondering the Principles

1. Review the section on the right attitude to have about money (see pp. 8-9). Which of those attitudes do you presently have? Which do you lack? Choose the area in which you have the most difficulty. Use a concordance or topical Bible to see what God teaches about that attitude. For example, if you struggle most with being proud of your possessions, find out what the Bible says about pride. Ask God for wisdom in applying what you learn to your overall attitude about money.

2. Review the section on how to know if you love money (see pp. 10-11). Based on those five determining factors, do you love money? If so, you need to confess that to God and repent of it. All five factors show how a person who doesn't love money acts. Begin to do the opposite of what you have done in the past. Strive for excellence in your work, be satisfied with what you have, don't flaunt what God has given you, give away money sacrificially, and don't sin to get more money.

3. Review the section on how to be content (see pp. 18-19). If you haven't already begun to apply those principles in your life, start today. Consider making a list of what you own, with your name on top. When the list is complete, cross out your name and write "God's" in its place. Then specifically thank God for everything on that list. From now on, carefully plan your trips

to the store. The only things that should be on your list are those which you actually need and can afford. Don't get caught in the trap of spending more than you make. Finally, determine what you can afford to give to the Lord's work and then try to give a little more than that. You will be making a sacrifice that will reap eternal rewards.

2
Avoiding the Love of Money

Outline

Introduction

Lesson
I. The Proper Treasury (vv. 19-21)
   A. The Perspectives
      1. Earthly treasure
         a) The definition
         b) The interpretation
      2. Heavenly treasure
   B. The Problem
   C. The Principle
II. The Proper Vision (vv. 22-23)
   A. Spiritual Perception
      1. Clear eyes
      2. Blind eyes
   B. Sincere Generosity
III. The Proper Allegiance (v. 24)
   A. The Commands of the Masters
   B. The Sovereignty of God
      1. God owns everything
      2. God controls everything
      3. God provides everything
IV. The Proper Confidence (vv. 25-34)
   A. The Principle (v. 25)
      1. The needlessness of worry
      2. The necessities of life

B. The Protection (vv. 26-32, 34)
  1. Worry is unnecessary because of our Father (vv. 26-30)
    a) The illustrations
      (1) Food (v. 26)
      (2) Life (v. 27)
      (3) Clothing (vv. 28-30a)
        (a) The anxiety
        (b) The analogy
        (c) The argument
    b) The indictment (v. 30b)
  2. Worry is uncharacteristic because of our faith (vv. 31-32)
  3. Worry is unwise because of our future (v. 34)
C. The Priority (v. 33)
  1. Seek the conversion of the lost
  2. Fulfill the commands of God
  3. Anticipate the return of Christ

Introduction

In 1 Timothy 6:10 the apostle Paul says, "The love of money is the root of all evil, which, while some coveted after, they have erred from the faith, and pierced themselves through with many sorrows." In the last chapter we looked at the danger of loving money. Now we need to learn how to avoid loving money. The best text for that is Matthew 6:19-34. In that passage our Lord teaches us how to avoid being preoccupied with material things.

To eliminate any love for money we must have the proper treasury, the proper vision, the proper allegiance, and the proper confidence.

Lesson

I. THE PROPER TREASURY (vv. 19-21)

"Lay not up for yourselves treasures upon earth, where moth and rust doth corrupt, and where thieves break through and steal, but lay up for yourselves treasures in heaven, where neither moth nor rust doth corrupt, and where thieves do not break through nor steal; for where your treasure is, there will your heart be also."

A. The Perspectives

Where do you invest your money?

1. Earthly treasure

   a) The definition

   Another way to translate verse 19 is: "treasure not up for yourselves treasure." The Greek word translated "treasure" (*thēsaurizete*) gives us the English word *thesaurus*, which refers to a treasury of words. *Thēsaurizete* means "to lay aside," "to store," or "to horde." Some lexicons indicate that it refers to a vertical stacking of things.

   b) The interpretation

   The Lord is not forbidding us to earn money or to keep money for good purposes. Rather He is forbidding us to store money to waste on our own self-indulgence. When people perceive life as a pursuit of money to be stored and used for their own selfish reasons, they have the wrong perspective. The key words in verse 19 are "for yourselves." Jesus didn't say, "Lay not up treasures upon earth," but, "Lay not up for yourselves treasures upon earth."

   The sin Jesus referred to has nothing to do with earning or saving money. Proverbs 21:20 implies that we should save money. In the parable of the talents Jesus implied that the least we should do is to put our money in the bank to earn interest (Matt. 25:27). The sin our Lord addressed in Matthew 6:19 is the sin of materialism, which is the accumulation of wealth for the purpose of self-indulgence, and also hard-heartedness toward the will of God.

   The Lord never condemns money itself, nor does He condemn the possession of it. In fact, it is God who gives us the power to get wealth (Deut. 8:18). He makes some people wealthy and others poor. God richly provides all things for us to enjoy (1 Tim. 6:17). Abraham was a rich man who was called the friend of God (James 2:23). God twice made Job wealthy, the second time giving him twice as much as the first (Job 42:10). The New Testament extols diligence in business (Rom. 12:11) and provision for one's household (1 Tim. 5:8). However, we sin when we invest the money God has given us in ourselves instead of in the kingdom of heaven.

2. Heavenly treasure

In Matthew 6:20 Jesus says, "Lay up for yourselves treasure in heaven." When we lay up treasure for ourselves on earth, it will remain here after we die. But when we lay up treasure for ourselves in heaven, it will be there to greet us when we arrive. All our efforts and gifts toward the advancement of the Lord's kingdom and the glory of His name constitute heavenly treasury.

a) Luke 16:9—Jesus said, "Make to yourselves friends by means of the money of unrighteousness, that, when it fails, they may receive you into everlasting habitations." Money is unrighteous in the sense that it isn't righteous—it has no righteous value inherent in it. In a sense, Jesus was saying to use money to buy friendships. The key is in understanding the kind of friendships we purchase: friends who will receive us "into everlasting habitations." We're to invest our money in the souls of men and women who will someday greet us in heaven with thanksgiving. We can purchase eternal friendships by investing in the kingdom. What we keep for ourselves, we lose; what we give to God, we keep forever.

b) Colossians 3:2—"Set your affection on things above, not on things on the earth."

B. The Problem

If we lay up treasure on earth, we will run into problems. In ancient Israel treasure meant basically three things: garments (one's clothes), grain (one's crop), and gold (one's

30

monetary fortune). In Matthew 6:19 Jesus stated the problems: "Where moth and rust doth corrupt, and where thieves break through and steal." Moths will eat your clothes. The Greek word translated "rust" (*brosis*) actually means "eating" and in this context refers to rats and other vermin that would eat stored grain. Many of the homes in that day were made of mud, and thieves would "break through" the wall and steal a person's money. The lesson is applicable today: if you put your fortune in worldly things, it is subject to worldly corruption.

C. The Principle

Verse 20 tells us that there's no need for mothballs in heaven. Nothing can corrupt what you lay aside there. And there are no thieves in heaven. The main thing Jesus wanted us to understand is asserted in verse 21: "Where your treasure is, there will your heart be also." Rather than spending what you have on purposeless consumption and self-indulgence, give it to the Lord. Then your fortune will be with God and you'll have a heart for His kingdom. Where is your treasury? If you love money, it's only here. If you love God more than you love money, your treasury is in heaven.

II. THE PROPER VISION (vv. 22-23)

"The lamp of the body is the eye; if, therefore, thine eye be healthy, thy whole body shall be full of light. But if thine eye be evil, thy whole body shall be full of darkness. If, therefore, the light that is in thee be darkness, how great is that darkness!"

A. Spiritual Perception

Just as your eyes affect your physical perception, so the focus of your heart determines your spiritual perception.

1. Clear eyes

Through your eyes, light is able to enter your body. There is no other means by which you can perceive light. The same is true of spiritually clear eyes—they can

31

see because they focus on the kingdom of heaven. The heart set on godly things has spiritual sight.

2. Blind eyes

Blind eyes see only darkness. An earthly perspective plunges one into spiritual darkness. If your focus is continually on accumulating money to indulge yourself, you are blind to spiritual reality. Your vision will be clouded by a severe darkness (v. 23). Greedy people become blind to spiritual reality. They can't determine spiritual needs or see the value of spiritual investments.

B. Sincere Generosity

The Greek word translated "healthy" in verse 22 means "generous."

The word translated "evil" (*ponēros*) is used as well in Deuteronomy 15:9 in the Septuagint (the Greek translation of the Old Testament) to refer to someone who is grudging or stingy. So Paul is saying that if you are characteristically generous in putting your treasure in heaven, you'll have clear spiritual vision. But if you tend to be stingy and invest your money only in yourself, you are spiritually blind. Generosity reflects a clear understanding of life; selfishness distorts spiritual vision.

III. THE PROPER ALLEGIANCE (v. 24)

"No man can serve two masters; for either he will hate the one, and love the other; or else he will hold to the one, and despise the other. Ye cannot serve God and money."

A. The Commands of the Masters

Love for money is exclusive—it eliminates love for God. To love the Lord your God with all your heart, soul, mind, and strength is to put away your love for money. The orders you receive from God are diametrically opposed to the ones you obey when you are ruled by a self-indulgent love for money. One master commands you to walk by faith, the other to walk by sight. One calls you to be humble, the other to be proud. One tells you to set your affection on

32

things above, the other to set it on things of the earth. One asks you to look at things unseen and eternal, the other at things seen and temporal. One tells you not to worry about anything, the other to worry about everything. One commands you to be content with what you have, the other to enlarge your desires. One calls you to share what you have with the needy, the other to withhold it from them. One wants you to be concerned about others, the other to be concerned about yourself. One asks you to seek happiness in the Creator, the other to seek happiness in the creature. Those two masters are mutually exclusive. You must determine to which you will give your allegiance.

B. The Sovereignty of God

Know that the safest place for your money is with God. He's the most faithful steward of all. Sadly, we live in a world gone mad over the accumulation of money for selfish purposes. Man indulges himself under the illusion that money brings happiness, joy, peace, and contentment. It doesn't. Contentment is the result of being attached to the right master.

1. God owns everything

Psalm 24:1 says, "The earth is the Lord's." First Chronicles 29:11 says, "All that is in the heaven and in the earth is thine." It all belongs to Him. The nation of Israel knew that God owns everything. They saw themselves as His stewards and managed His possessions for Him. In contrast we have adopted the mentality of the Egyptian, Greek, and Roman cultures, who believed they were the true owners of their possessions.

2. God controls everything

First Chronicles 29:11-12 implies that God controls everything.

3. God provides everything

God has given us everything we have. We possess nothing that God has not allowed us to possess. Luke 12:31-34 says, "Seek ye the kingdom of God, and all

33

these things shall be added unto you. Fear not, little flock; for it is your Father's good pleasure to give you the kingdom. Sell what ye have, and give alms; provide yourselves bags which grow not old, a treasure in the heavens that faileth not, where no thief approacheth, neither moth corrupteth. For where your treasure is, there will your heart be also." If God wants you to give away everything He has given you, you can be secure, knowing He is in charge of providing what you need.

You don't have to control your destiny. If the Spirit of God prompts your heart, respond to Him with the confidence that God owns everything, controls everything, and promises to provide everything you need. Since God gave you life, He will sustain you.

Bread in the Children's Hands

As World War II came to a close, the Allied armies gathered together many of the orphans left by the war. They were placed in camps where they were well fed. Despite the excellent care, I remember reading that the children had difficulty sleeping. They were nervous and afraid. Psychologists were brought in to determine the cause of the children's sleeplessness. They came up with this solution: every night before the children were put in bed, they were each given a little piece of bread to hold in their hands. It worked! The children went to sleep, clutching their little pieces of bread.

Why couldn't the children sleep? Apparently they had lived so long in a state of uncertainty that they couldn't sleep for fear they wouldn't be able to find food the next day. Once they had those little pieces of bread in their hands, they had some security for the next day and were able to sleep. God has given us this wonderful promise: "Fear not, little flock; for it is your Father's good pleasure to give you the kingdom" (Luke 12:32). He has put little pieces of bread in our hands so we can sleep. What is there to be worried about?

IV. THE PROPER CONFIDENCE (vv. 25-34)

A. The Principle (v. 25)

"Therefore, I say unto you, Be not anxious for your life, what ye shall eat, or what ye shall drink; nor yet for your body, what ye shall put on. Is not the life more than food and the body than raiment?"

"Be not anxious" is something Jesus was compelled to repeat two more times (vv. 31, 34). The people were excessively worried about things they ought not to have been worried about. In verse 25 the Greek tense indicates that they needed to stop being anxious, whereas verse 31 says they ought not to start being anxious. Jesus wanted them to stop being anxious about their lives (Gk., *psuchē*)—their physical, earthly lives.

1. The needlessness of worry

Among those who want to give to the kingdom, develop spiritual vision, and give their allegiance to God are those who remain concerned about providing for themselves. They don't understand that God doesn't want them to give away the necessities for life; He just does not want them to think they must amass a fortune to cover all the bases in life. When the Holy Spirit attempts to prompt such people to give, they don't, and thus are disobeying God.

Our Lord was saying that heavenly treasure puts our hearts in the right place, generous giving gives us spiritual vision, and allegiance to the Lord puts us under His loving authority and care; and for those reasons we can have the confidence and freedom not to worry about our physical life.

2. The necessities of life

Even the necessities of life are under God's control. In verse 25 Jesus says, "Be not anxious for your life, what ye shall eat, or what ye shall drink; nor yet for your body, what ye shall put on. Is not the life more than

35

food and the body than raiment?" Don't be preoccupied with material things.

Hebrews 13:5 says you are to "be content with such things as ye have." God may want us to invest everything we have beyond the necessities of life in His kingdom, perhaps by giving to someone in need. We need to be prepared to respond without fear to whatever He asks because we have the confidence that we're in His care. That's what it means to live by faith.

B. The Protection (vv. 26-32, 34)

The necessities in life which Christ referred to are food, water, and clothing. The pursuit of those things could occupy a great deal of our time. But Jesus said that we need not worry about them for the following reasons.

1. Worry is unnecessary because of our Father (vv. 26-30)

    God promises to take care of our needs.

    a) The illustrations

        (1) Food (v. 26)

            "Behold the fowls of the air; for they sow not, neither do they reap, nor gather into barns, yet your heavenly Father feedeth them. Are ye not much better than they?"

            (a) Job 38:41—"Who provideth for the raven his prey?"

            (b) Psalm 104:25, 27—"So is this great and wide sea, wherein are things creeping innumerable, both small and great beasts. . . . These all wait upon thee, that thou mayest give them their food in due season." God feeds all creation—doesn't that include you? Indeed, man is the crown of His creation.

(2) Life (v. 27)

"Which of you by being anxious can add one cubit unto his stature?"

A cubit is eighteen inches. However, Christ is not referring to a person's height. If He were, He would have been saying that I want to be seven feet ten inches tall! The Greek word translated "stature" (*hēlikia*) refers to a person's span of life. Actually Jesus was saying, "Which of you can worry yourself into a longer life?"

However, the converse may be true: if you worry about your life, you're likely to have a shorter one. Charles Mayo observed in the medical journal *American Mercury* that worry affects the circulatory system, the heart, the glands, and the entire nervous system. He said he never knew a man to die of overwork but knew of many who died of worry. You can worry yourself to death, but you'll never worry yourself into a longer life.

Such worry is ultimately the sin of refusing to trust God, and that is foolish. God has given you life and will allow you to live as long as He wants you to within His sovereign plan. There's no way you can lengthen that time. However, you can shorten it by sinning (e.g., 1 Cor. 15:30; 1 John 5:16-17). The length of your life will be the full span that God sovereignly designed. So why not live it to His glory? You don't need to control your destiny; you need to invest your life in God's kingdom as prompted by the Spirit. Let Him take care of the results. You just might see Him provide you with more than you can possibly use, because He is a God of grace.

(3) Clothing (vv. 28-30*a*)

"Why are ye anxious for raiment? Consider the lilies of the field, how they grow; they toil not, neither do they spin, and yet I say unto you that even Solomon, in all his glory, was not arrayed like one of these. Wherefore, if God so clothe the grass of the field, which today is, and tomorrow is cast into the oven, shall he not much more clothe you?"

(a) The anxiety

Some people are anxious about the clothes they wear. They don't want to leave home if they have to wear the same thing they wore the day before. Some working mothers leave their children with others for no better reason than to support certain fashion habits. Lusting after costly clothes is sin. First Timothy 2:9 says that women should "adorn themselves in modest apparel." First Peter 3:4 says that adorning should be internal: "Let it be the hidden man of the heart in that which is not corruptible, even the ornament of a meek and quiet spirit." Those qualities characterized Sarah (v. 6).

(b) The analogy

We don't have to worry about clothes because the Lord promised to clothe us beautifully. He used field lilies to illustrate that promise. The royal garments of King Solomon paled in comparison to the magnificence of those wildflowers. When viewed under the close scrutiny of a microscope, the finest fabric that man has created looks just like burlap. But put a flower under a microscope and you will see the delicate beauty of God's creation. There's no comparison. The scarlet poppies that blossom on the hillsides of Israel are clothed in a beauty that far surpasses the royal robes of kings. A day later the flowers are burned up by the sun, but they are soon replaced by new ones equal in beauty.

(c) The argument

> In verse 30 Christ says, "If God so clothe the grass of the field, which today is, and tomorrow is cast into the oven, shall he not much more clothe you?" I'm not going to stop giving to God because I'm afraid I might not have enough to buy a new suit. I want to give all I have to God and let Him clothe me.

b) The indictment (v. 30*b*)

"O ye of little faith."

That's the basic problem, and it certainly was characteristic of the disciples. They weren't to worry about the necessities of life; they were to trust their Lord to meet those needs. Living by faith doesn't necessarily mean you'll live in poverty. But it does mean you accept what God gives you, and you invest it in His kingdom.

2. Worry is uncharacteristic because of our faith (vv. 31-32)

"Therefore, be not anxious saying, What shall we eat? or, What shall we drink? or, With what shall we be clothed? For after all these things do the Gentiles seek. For your heavenly Father knoweth that ye have need of all these things."

God knows exactly what we need. Our task is to seek "first the kingdom of God, and his righteousness, and all these things shall be added unto you" (v. 33). I'm not to be anxious about what I eat, what I drink, or what I put on because that attitude is typical of unbelievers. They're worried about those things. But for me worry is needless because of God's bounty, senseless because of God's promise, and useless because of man's weakness.

I want to see God work in my life. Do you trust God to do things that you know only He can do? When He does those things, do you give Him all the credit? Some of us are insulated from seeing God do anything for us because we want to have every base covered—"just in case." Where is your vulnerability so that God can work in your life? Only by faith can we see His hand at work, and our faith is well placed in God, because He loves and cares for His own.

Unbelievers, however, have no connection to God, so they amass belongings for themselves. The emphatic use of the Greek word translated "seek" in verse 32 indicates that they are consumed with material gratification. Some people believe that materialism is a trivial sin, but I believe it is very serious because it strikes at the character and promise of God. Materialistic people reject God as the loving provider for His own.

What are we to seek? "The kingdom of God, and his righteousness" (v. 33a). When we seek first His kingdom, He provides for our needs (v. 33b). That's the only way to live. Don't love money; love God. Don't seek money; seek God. And don't seek to be rich; seek to do your best.

3. Worry is unwise because of our future (v. 34)

"Be, therefore, not anxious about tomorrow; for tomorrow will be anxious for the things of itself. Sufficient unto the day is its own evil."

We need not worry about tomorrow because God is the God of tomorrow. Tomorrow will be whatever it will be, but God will be as faithful then as He is today. The worries of tomorrow will still be there tomorrow, but so will God. Instead of worrying, you ought to live for today.

Worrying about the future debilitates many people. As a result, they forfeit the joy of today because they sentence themselves to anxiety about an unknown future. The Lord urges us not to do that because tomorrow will have enough trouble of its own. You don't need tomorrow's troubles added to today's. God gives you the strength you need for today—no more, but no less. Lamentations 3:23 says His mercies "are new every morning; great is thy faithfulness." Fear is a liar. It doesn't tell the truth about the future. Don't cripple the present by worrying about the future.

C. The Priority (v. 33)

"Seek ye first the kingdom of God, and his righteousness, and all these things shall be added unto you."

What did Christ mean specifically by that?

1. Seek the conversion of the lost

   Entrance into the kingdom of God is by grace through faith in Christ (Eph. 2:8). Therefore we extend the kingdom by leading others to Christ.

2. Fulfill the commands of God

   Romans 14:17 says, "The kingdom of God is not food and drink, but righteousness, and peace, and joy in the Holy Spirit." We are to reflect the righteous character of the kingdom in our lives.

3. Anticipate the return of Christ

   We're also to anticipate the coming millennial reign of Christ, which ultimately ushers in His eternal kingdom (1 Thess. 1:10).

We are to seek the kingdom in every sense. With our energies, talents, time, and money—with every aspect of our lives we are to promote the advance of God's kingdom. If God responds by giving you much or little, be content knowing that your needs will be met. Christ said that if you seek the kingdom, all those earthly "things shall be added unto you" (Matt. 6:33). Allow yourself the privilege of living under the promises of God.

Focusing on the Facts

1. What did the Lord forbid believers to do in Matthew 6:19 (see p. 29)?
2. What does Scripture teach about having wealth (see pp. 29-30)?
3. How can believers give money to God yet have it reap dividends for themselves (see p. 30)?

41

4. Why did Jesus say that we should use money to make friends (Luke 16:9; see p. 30)?
5. What happens when we invest our money in worldly things (see p. 31)?
6. Explain the difference between spiritually clear and blind eyes (Matt. 6:22-23; see pp. 31-32).
7. What does the love of money eliminate? Explain (see pp. 32-33).
8. Why can we be secure even if God asks us to give away everything we possess (see p. 34)?
9. Explain why it is needless for believers to worry about their physical lives (see p. 35).
10. What are the three necessities of life that believers need not worry about (see pp. 35-36)?
11. Can a person worry himself into a longer life? Explain (Matt. 6:27; see p. 37).
12. How do the finest clothes compare to the flowers God created (see p. 38)?
13. How can a believer see God work in his life (see pp. 39-40)?
14. Why is materialism such a serious sin (see p. 40)?
15. Why does worry about the future debilitate people (see p. 40)?
16. What did Christ specifically mean when He told us to seek God's kingdom (see p. 41)?

Pondering the Principles

1. Where is your heart? Is your life centered on the things you own or on God? Make a list of the different things you do during the week. Next to each item, note whether that time is spent for you or for God. Based on that analysis, how do you spend the majority of your time? Do you need to spend more time concentrating on heavenly things? Take one of the items from your list, and stop spending that time on yourself. Instead, make it your priority this week to invest that time in God. Do that with another item next week, and keep up the practice until you are in the habit of continually spending meaningful time on the things of the Lord.

2. Is anxiety a regular part of your life? Make a list of the various things you worry about. How many of them come under the category of necessities such as food, clothing, and shelter? According to Matthew 6:33 those things are not your concern, but

God's. What are you to be preoccupied with? How much of the day do you spend thinking about heavenly things? Start alleviating your anxiety by memorizing the simple priority and promise that Jesus gives us in Matthew 6:33: "Seek first His kingdom and His righteousness; and all these things shall be added to you" (NASB*).

* *New American Standard Bible.*

3
The Man of God

Outline

Introduction
A. Identifying Timothy as a Man of God
  1. The title
     a) Its use in the Old Testament
     b) Its use in the New Testament
  2. The task
B. Reminding Timothy of His Calling

Lesson
  I. What He Flees From (v. 11*a*)
     A. The Context
     B. The Example
 II. What He Follows After (v. 11*b*)
     A. General Virtues
        1. Righteousness
        2. Godliness
     B. Specific Virtues
        1. Faith
        2. Love
        3. Patience
        4. Meekness
III. What He Fights For (v. 12)
     A. The Nature of the Fight
        1. A lifelong fight
        2. An agonizing fight
        3. A good fight
     B. The Motive of the Fight
        1. The call
        2. The confession

IV. What He Is Faithful To (vv. 13-14)
   A. Grasping the Commandment
   B. Guarding the Commandment
     1. The power
     2. The cost
       a) God's protection
       b) Christ's example
     3. The commitment
       a) Total faithfulness
       b) Ongoing faithfulness

Conclusion

Introduction

One of my favorite biblical phrases is "man of God." It appears in 1 Timothy 6:11 as a title the apostle Paul gave to Timothy. What a privilege—to be called a man of God! It is a possessive phrase indicating that Timothy belonged to God in a unique way.

A. Identifying Timothy as a Man of God

  1. The title

While "man of God" is a common descriptive phrase in the Old Testament, it is uncommon in the New. Only one person in the New Testament is called a man of God, and that is Timothy. Paul conferred the title on him to increase his sense of responsibility in ministry. When you are reminded that you belong to God, it's difficult to avoid the weight of responsibility that comes with it.

a) Its use in the Old Testament

The prophets were frequently referred to as men of God. They represented Him by speaking His truth. By calling Timothy a "man of God," Paul was emphasizing his responsibility to speak the truth of God.

46

b) Its use in the New Testament

    (1) 2 Peter 1:21—This refers back to the Old Testament men of God: "The prophecy came not at any time by the will of man, but holy men of God spoke as they were moved by the Holy Spirit."

    (2) 2 Timothy 3:16-17—Every use of "man of God" in Scripture is specific except for its broad use here: "All scripture is given by inspiration of God, and is profitable for doctrine, for reproof, for correction, for instruction in righteousness, that the man of God may be perfect, thoroughly furnished unto all good works." At first glance verse 17 appears to refer to Timothy since he was the recipient of the letter and since Paul refers to his conversion in verses 14-15. But actually it applies to any man of God, especially one who articulates God's Word.

Since 2 Timothy 3:17 uses "man of God" in a generic sense, we are not reluctant to broaden its use to encompass anyone today who is a spokesman for God. He has always had His spokesmen, whether they be prophets or preachers. The man of God can be anyone who, having been matured by the Word, is called to proclaim the Word.

2. The task

Paul's instruction to Timothy is heightened and intensified as Timothy is identified with the long line of historic spokesmen for God. As John Bunyan implied in *The Pilgrim's Progress*, the man of God is "the King's champion" ([N.Y.: Pocket Books, 1957], p. 125). Men of God are lifted above worldly aims to be devoted to divine service. They are not the world's men, nor are they their own men—they are God's men.

B. Reminding Timothy of His Calling

Timothy was faced with an important ministry in Ephesus. Paul left him there to bring order to a church that had been infiltrated by false doctrine and false teachers. They were teaching heresy and tolerating sin. Three times in this epistle Paul explained to Timothy how to respond to false teachers. On each occasion he reminded Timothy of the sacredness of his calling.

1. 1 Timothy 1:18—"This charge I commit unto thee, son Timothy, according to the prophecies which pointed to thee."

2. 1 Timothy 4:14—"Neglect not the gift that is in thee, which was given thee by prophecy, with the laying on of the hands of the presbytery."

3. 1 Timothy 6:12—"Fight the good fight of faith, lay hold on eternal life, unto which thou art also called and hast professed a good profession before many witnesses."

Lesson

First Timothy 6:11 says, "But thou, O man of God." The phrase translated "but thou" contrasts Timothy with the false teachers mentioned in verses 3-10. Timothy belonged to God, whereas the false teachers belonged to money, materialism, the world, sin, and Satan. The Greek word translated "O" is a personal, emotional appeal. Its use is rare in personal greetings in Greek. It reveals the pleading nature of Paul's heart. Paul begged Timothy to remember his spiritual calling and not to lose sight of his identity.

What identifies a man of God? Four things: what he flees from, what he follows after, what he fights for, and what he is faithful to.

I. WHAT HE FLEES FROM (v. 11a)

"But thou, O man of God, flee these things."

That's a present imperative: be continually fleeing. The Greek word translated "flee" is *pheugō*, from which we derive the English word *fugitive*—someone who escapes a pursuer. The Greeks used it to refer to someone running from a plague, a poisonous snake, or an attacking enemy. The man of God does not stand still; he is known by what he flees from. In 1 Corinthians 6:18 Paul says, "Flee fornication." First Corinthians

10:14 says, "Flee from idolatry." In 2 Timothy 2:22 Paul says to Timothy, "Flee also youthful lusts."

A. The Context

In 1 Timothy 6:11 Paul says, "Flee these things." What things? The things he had just discussed—the evils attached to loving money. Verses 9-10 say, "They that will be rich fall into temptation and a snare, and into many foolish and hurtful lusts, which drown men in destruction and perdition. For the love of money is the root of all evil, which, while some coveted after, they have erred from the faith, and pierced themselves through with many sorrows." So Paul was urging Timothy to flee from the love of money and all its attendant griefs, lusts, and temptations. The man of God does not have an affection for material things.

Paul had already warned Timothy to avoid several things: endless genealogies (1 Tim. 1:4), fables (4:7), and vain babblings and so-called knowledge (6:20). Here he says to flee the love of money, which is the root of all kinds of evil. Greed motivates false teachers who pervert the truth for personal gain. To them people are only a means to accomplish their ends.

They are like the false prophet Balaam, who was bought by the highest bidder (Num. 22-24), and Judas, who sold Jesus for thirty pieces of silver (Matt. 27:1-10). They are like the false prophets of Israel, who were "greedy dogs that can never have enough . . . they all look to their own way, every one for his gain" (Isa. 56:11). They include the covetous prophets and priests of Jeremiah's time (Jer. 6:13); the prophets of Ezekiel's time, who could be bought with handfuls of barley and pieces of bread (Ezek. 13:19); and the prophets of Micah's time, who divined for money (Mic. 3:11). Then there are the false teachers who spoke "good words" and gave "fair speeches" to the Roman church to satisfy their bodily lusts (Rom. 16:18). And they are like the "unruly and vain talkers and deceivers" of Crete, who subverted "whole houses, teaching things which they ought not, for filthy lucre's sake" (Titus 1:10-11). The characteristic of false teachers is greed, but that is not characteristic of the man of God.

B. The Example

Paul was careful to avoid the love of money.

1. Acts 20:33-34—To the Ephesian elders Paul said, "I have coveted no man's silver, or gold, or apparel. Yea, ye yourselves know that these hands have ministered unto my necessities, and to them that were with me."

2. 1 Corinthians 9:14-15—Paul acknowledged that preachers had a right to make a living from their ministry: "Even so hath the Lord ordained that they who preach the gospel should live of the gospel" (v. 14). Nevertheless he refused to claim that right so that the people wouldn't think he was preaching for money (v. 15).

3. Philippians 2:20-21—Paul said, "I have no man likeminded, who will naturally care for your state. For all seek their own, not the things which are Jesus Christ's." The only person Paul could send them was Timothy (v. 19). Paul had to contend with many people like Demas, who "having loved this present world" forsook the ministry (2 Tim. 4:10).

4. 1 Thessalonians 2:7, 9—To the Thessalonian church Paul could say, "We were gentle among you, even as a nurse cherisheth her children. . . . Ye remember, brethren, our labor and travail; for laboring night and day, because we would not be chargeable unto any of you."

You may call yourself a preacher, but if you're in the ministry for the money, you're not a man of God. Instead you have prostituted the call of God. Never put a price on your ministry. Whatever you charge will have the net effect of devaluing your ministry to nothing.

II. WHAT HE FOLLOWS AFTER (v. 11b)

"Follow after righteousness, godliness, faith, love, patience, meekness."

While continually avoiding evil things, the man of God continually pursues what is good. That's implied in the present imperative verb translated "to follow after." Like the widow who "diligently followed every good work" (5:10), the man of God pursues what is right.

We can never stop running as long as we're alive. If we stop running from what is evil, it will catch us. If we cease pursuing what is righteous, it will elude us. While on earth we will never arrive at the point where we finally outdistance what is wrong or fully capture what is right.

In 2 Timothy 2:22 Paul says, "Flee also youthful lusts, but follow righteousness, faith, love, peace." Proverbs 15:9 says the Lord "loveth him that followeth after righteousness." What do you pursue? Do you want to attain success, fame, esteem, promotion, money, and possessions? A man of God follows after righteousness, godliness, faith, love, endurance, and meekness.

A. General Virtues

The first two virtues are overarching—the first deals with external behavior and the second with internal attitude and motivation.

1. Righteousness

The Greek word translated "righteousness" (*dikaiosune*) refers to acting correctly toward God and man. Isaiah referred to the faithful remnant of Israel as "Ye that follow after righteousness" (51:1). The writer of Hebrews said, "Follow peace with all men, and holiness, without which no man shall see the Lord" (12:14).

In 1 Timothy 6:11 Paul is not referring to imputed righteousness, which is the righteousness one receives positionally in Christ at salvation. Instead he is referring to practical righteousness. The man of God is known by his doing right. He obeys God's standard and resists temptation.

2. Godliness

Righteousness refers to one's behavior; godliness refers to one's attitude and motivation. Here Paul directs our thoughts toward reverence, holiness, and piety. The

Greek word translated "godliness" (*eusebeia*) is used nine times in the pastoral epistles. Godliness is a rich theme that Paul uses throughout those three letters. Right behavior flows out of a right attitude; right action flows out of right motives. A godly person, in the words of Hebrews 12:28, serves "God acceptably with reverence and godly fear." He lives life conscious of God's holiness.

Paul was so concerned with matters of godliness that he said to the Ephesian elders, "Take heed, therefore, unto yourselves" (Acts 20:28). He said to Timothy, "Take heed unto thyself" (1 Tim. 4:16). And he wrote to Timothy that if he wanted to be "a vessel unto honor, sanctified, and fit for the master's use" he needed to purge himself (2 Tim. 2:21). We need to keep checking what's inside.

The two overarching virtues the man of God pursues are righteousness and godliness. They are at the core of his usefulness and power. Watch your motives, desires, conduct, and behavior.

B. Specific Virtues

1. Faith

Faith is confident trust and belief in God. The man of God lives by faith. He trusts our sovereign God to keep His Word and meet his needs.

2. Love

The Greek word translated "love" (*agapē*) speaks of volitional love. It is the love of unrestricted and unrestrained choice, and it encompasses God, Christians, and non-Christians alike. He who loves with that volitional love understands what it is to love the Lord with all his heart, soul, mind, and strength and his neighbor as himself. He loves God and others more than he loves himself. He loves others enough to confront them with the truth. Don't pretend to love someone whose sins you are not willing to confront.

3. Patience

The Greek word translated "patience" (*hupomonē*) means "to remain under." It doesn't refer to a passive resignation, but to a victorious, triumphant endurance—an unswerving loyalty to the Lord in the midst of trials. Patience is the endurance of a martyr who will give his life if need be, or the forbearance of the shepherd who lays down his life for his flock. It's the ability to endure injustice, deprivation, pain, grief, and even death with spiritual staying power. Second Corinthians 11 catalogs all that Paul triumphantly endured.

4. Meekness

Another word for meekness is humility. The humble person is not self-oriented. Though consumed with a great cause, he does not think of himself as being a key contributor to its success.

The man of God is known by his right behavior, right motives and thoughts, confidence in God, love toward God and men, endurance, and humility, no matter what the circumstances are.

III. WHAT HE FIGHTS FOR (v. 12)

"Fight the good fight of faith, lay hold on eternal life, unto which thou art also called and hast professed a good profession before many witnesses."

A. The Nature of the Fight

1. A lifelong fight

The man of God sees himself as a fighter. He is engaged in an ongoing war of truth against error.

a) 2 Timothy 2:3-4—"Endure hardness, as a good soldier of Jesus Christ. No man that warreth entangleth himself with the affairs of this life, that he may please him who hath chosen him to be a soldier."

b) 2 Timothy 4:7—When Paul came to the end of his ministry he said, "I have fought a good fight."

To perceive the ministry as anything less than a battle is to lose the fight. We battle the world, the flesh, and the devil (1 John 2:16). We also battle sin, heresy, error, apathy, and lethargy in the church.

2. An agonizing fight

The Greek verb translated "fight" (*agōnizomai*) implies that we're to fight continually. It is used in both military and athletic contexts to describe the concentration, effort, and discipline needed to win. *Agōnizomai*, from which we get the English word *agonize*, is used repeatedly in the New Testament. We are to agonize through our spiritual conflict with sin, unrighteousness, and the kingdom of Satan.

I'm thrilled to be a soldier. People recognize that I usually am engaged in battle on some front. That's the way it ought to be. The prevailing notion that one should set aside any doctrinal teaching with which others disagree is frightening! We are to earnestly contend for the faith in spite of the intensity and danger inherent in war.

3. A good fight

Paul says to "fight the good [Gk., *kalos*, "excellent," "noble"] fight of faith." We are to engage in noble warfare to preserve the faith as revealed in Scripture. That's the highest cause in the world. Don't compromise; instead, fight effectively.

B. The Motive of the Fight

Those brave enough to fight will face certain trouble in this world. To balance the suffering Paul says, "Lay hold on eternal life, unto which thou art also called and hast professed a good profession before many witnesses" (v. 12).

That was Paul's way of saying, "Get a grip on eternal life." You won't mind suffering in this world as much if you live in the light of eternity. Any effort you exert in this short life for Christ's sake is recompensed immeasurably in eternity.

Colossians 3:2 says, "Set your affection on things above, not on things on the earth." Philippians 3:20 makes clear that "our citizenship is in heaven." We are to live and minister in the light of eternity. That enables us to keep our focus on the battle.

1. The call

Timothy was called to eternal life (1 Tim. 6:12) and was expected to live in light of that. In the epistles each use of the Greek word translated "called" refers to God's sovereign call to salvation or eternal life.

2. The confession

Paul reminded Timothy that he (Timothy) had publicly professed his faith in Christ "before many witnesses" (v. 12). Paul may have been referring to Timothy's baptism or his ordination. Since Timothy claimed to possess eternal life, he was to live in the light of that fact.

What would you think of a person who claimed to live for eternity yet spent everything he had striving to amass things here and now? Jesus said, "Where your treasure is, there will your heart be also" (Matt. 6:21). The man of God divorces himself from this world and lives in the light of eternity.

Paul continued to minister because he knew that some day he would stand before Jesus Christ. He lived in the light of eternity. In Acts 1:11, after Jesus ascended to heaven, two angels said to the disciples, "This same Jesus, who is taken up from you into heaven, shall so come in like manner as ye have seen him go into heaven." The message of the angels was, "Get to work; He will be back soon." In 1 Timothy 4:8 Paul says, "Bodily exercise profiteth little, but godliness is profitable unto all things, having promise of the life that now is, and of that which is to come." Where are you going to spend your energies? On temporal things or eternal things? The man of God rises above pitiful strug-

55

gles for that which is perishable and ultimately useless. Instead he fights for the truth of God.

IV. WHAT HE IS FAITHFUL TO (vv. 13-14)

"I command thee in the sight of God, who maketh all things alive, and before Christ Jesus, who before Pontius Pilate witnessed a good confession, that thou keep this commandment without spot, unrebukable, until the appearing of our Lord Jesus Christ."

A. Grasping the Commandment

The main point is in verse 14: "Keep this commandment [Gk., *tēn entolēn*]." Some think the "commandment" is the gospel. Others believe it to be Paul's teaching in this epistle. Still others say it's the whole of the New Covenant. But "commandment" should be translated "the Word"; thus it is a reference to the complete revealed Word of God.

B. Guarding the Commandment

Paul commanded Timothy to "keep this commandment." He was to guard it with his life.

1. The power

In 2 Timothy 1:13-14 Paul says, "Hold fast the form of sound words. . . . That good thing which was committed unto thee keep by the Holy Spirit, who dwelleth in us." We depend on the Holy Spirit's power to uphold the truth in word and deed.

2. The cost

In 1 Timothy 6:13 Paul says, "I command thee in the sight of God." God is watching. That doesn't mean God is looking over your shoulder to clobber you if you make a mistake, but instead means that knowing that God is watching is an undeniable incentive to live a holy life.

We are to guard the truth in the sight of God, "who maketh all things alive" (v. 13). That refers to His resurrection. Paul's point is: keep the truth and don't waver.

Maintain the courage of your convictions and live by the truth even if you lose your life in the process. Why? Because God is watching, and He is able to raise the dead. The worst anyone can do to you is escort you into eternity.

a) God's protection

God not only creates life; He also sustains it. More than that, He restores life through His resurrection power. Millions of martyrs who died throughout the history of the church could surely attest to that now.

b) Christ's example

Paul then speaks of Jesus Christ, "who before Pontius Pilate witnessed a good confession" (1 Tim. 6:13). Pilate asked Christ if He was a king. Though it cost Him His life, Jesus confessed that He was. A man or woman of God tells the truth at any cost.

3. The commitment

a) Total faithfulness

In 1 Timothy 6:14 Paul says, "Keep this commandment without spot, unrebukable." Our lives are to be without blemish and without cause for accusation. We are to be totally faithful to the truth.

b) Ongoing faithfulness

Verse 14 concludes, "Until the appearing [Gk., *epiphainos*, "shining forth"] of our Lord Jesus Christ." That's how long we are to continue being faithful.

Conclusion

The man of God is known by what he flees from, follows after, fights for, and is faithful to. I thank God that in His grace He called me to preach His truth. But there's a risk.

First Kings 13 introduces us to an extraordinary man of God. Verse 1 says, "Behold, there came a man of God out of Judah by the word of the Lord unto Bethel." He was sent to prophesy against King Jeroboam, which he did (vv. 2-3). God had told him that once he had spoken the prophecy, he had to leave and could not eat or drink in Bethel (v. 9). But after an old prophet pled with him and deceived him, the man of God disobeyed (vv. 11-18). Verse 19 says, "[He] did eat bread in his house, and drank water." Eating and drinking is not a moral problem, but disobeying God is.

Verses 20-22 say, "It came to pass, as they sat at the table, that the word of the Lord came unto the prophet who brought him back; and he cried unto the man of God who came from Judah, saying, Thus saith the Lord, Forasmuch as thou hast disobeyed the mouth of the Lord, and hast not kept the commandment which the Lord thy God commanded thee, but camest back, and hast eaten bread and drunk water in the place, of which the Lord did say to thee, Eat no bread, and drink no water; thy carcass shall not come unto the sepulcher of thy fathers." When the man of God left the prophet's house, he was killed by a lion (v. 24). It's a wonderful privilege to be a man of God, but it's also a fearful responsibility. God expects us to keep His Word no matter what. There is potential for great blessing, but also for great danger.

Focusing on the Facts

1. Why did Paul refer to Timothy as a "man of God" (1 Tim. 6:11; see p. 46)?
2. How does Paul use the phrase "man of God" in 2 Timothy 3:17 (see p. 47)?
3. What did Paul remind Timothy of in telling him how to respond to false teachers (see pp. 47-48)?
4. What are some of the things the man of God is to flee? What does 1 Timothy 6:11 say to flee (see pp. 48-49)?
5. What was Paul's attitude toward money (see p. 50)?
6. What does the man of God pursue (see p. 51)?
7. Explain what righteousness is (see p. 51).
8. Describe a godly person (see p. 52).
9. Describe a person characterized by faith and love (see p. 52).
10. Define patience (see p. 53).
11. What is another word for meekness? Explain (see p. 53).

12. How is the man of God to see himself (1 Tim. 6:12)? Why (see pp. 53-54)?
13. What kind of fight is the man of God to be involved in? Explain (1 Tim. 6:12; see p. 54).
14. What is the motivation for suffering for Christ's sake (1 Tim. 6:12; see pp. 54-55)?
15. What does 1 Timothy 6:14 command us to do (see p. 56)?
16. How are we to keep that commandment (2 Tim. 1:13-14; see p. 56)?
17. Why can we confidently maintain the courage of our convictions and live out the truth even if our lives are threatened when we do so (1 Tim. 6:13; see p. 57)?
18. Explain Christ's example of guarding the truth (see p. 57).
19. What is the risk of being a man of God (see pp. 57-58)?

Pondering the Principles

1. Do you flee earthly possessions, or are you attracted by them? Read 1 Timothy 6:9-10. What dangers are associated with a love of money? In what way can the love of money hurt you? Make a list of all your possessions—even the small things. Next to each one, indicate whether it is a useful provision for your family or useful for serving the Lord. How many of the things on your list fall into neither category? In your honest estimation, are you materialistic? Go through your list once more Mentally transfer ownership of everything to God, who owns all you possess anyway. Thank Him for all He has given you—even for things that are strictly items of pleasure. Be willing to let go of anything He may decide to take away from you.

2. Review the section on what the man of God follows. Are you pursuing righteousness, godliness, faith, love, patience, and humility in your life? How would you rate the intensity of your pursuit in each of those areas—are you sprinting, running, jogging, walking, or completely immobile? Which virtue do you think is most important for you to quicken your pace in? Make a fresh commitment this week to a greater pursuit of that virtue. Ask God for His guidance in giving you specific opportunities to manifest that virtue.

4
A Solemn Call to Spiritual Duty

Outline

Introduction
A. The Necessity of Spiritual Duty
B. The Standard for Spiritual Duty
C. The Motivation for Spiritual Duty
D. The Hindrances to Spiritual Duty
    1. For Timothy
    2. For us
E. The Strength for Spiritual Duty

Lesson
I. The Power of God (vv. 13-14a)
    A. God Is the Creator of Life
    B. God Is the Sustainer of Life
    C. God Is the Preserver of Life
    D. God Is the Restorer of Life
        1. The principle explained
        2. The principle explored
        3. The principle illustrated
            a) The conspiracy against Christ
            b) The confession of Christ
            c) The confidence of Christ
II. The Truthfulness of God (vv. 14b-15a)
    A. The Explanation of His Promise
        1. Its source
        2. Its meaning
    B. The Vindication of His Son
    C. The Vindication of His People
    D. The Application of His Promise

Introduction

God calls every believer to spiritual duty, but the tasks He assigns will vary from person to person according to our abilities, giftedness, and opportunities for service. The degree to which we fulfill our duties is a measure of our commitment to Christ.

Timothy had enormous giftedness and opportunity for service, but he also needed encouragement from the apostle Paul to accomplish what God had called him to do.

A. The Necessity of Spiritual Duty

Timothy had a clear understanding of his call to spiritual duty. That call was affirmed by prophetic utterance when Paul and the Ephesian elders ordained him (1 Tim. 4:14; 2 Tim. 1:6), and most of his duties were assigned by Paul himself. In fact, 1 Timothy is a description of how he was to correct the problems that existed in the Ephesian church.

Although they were assigned by Paul, Timothy's spiritual duties were designed by God. That's why Paul admonished him to fulfill them in a faithful manner: "O man of God . . . follow after righteousness, godliness, faith, love, patience, meekness. Fight the good fight of faith, lay hold on eternal life, unto which thou art also called and hast professed a good profession before many witnesses" (1 Tim 6:11-12).

B. The Standard for Spiritual Duty

Paul said, "I was not disobedient unto the heavenly vision" (Acts 26:19). That is the standard for all spiritual duty. We're to obey immediately and willingly when God gives us something to do.

C. The Motivation for Spiritual Duty

Even though obedience is the standard for all spiritual duties, we all need to be stimulated from time to time. That was true for Timothy. Therefore Paul said, "I command thee in the sight of God, who maketh all things alive, and before Christ Jesus, who before Pontius Pilate witnessed a good confession, that thou keep this commandment without spot, unrebukable, until the appearing of our Lord Jesus Christ; which in his times he shall show, who is the blessed and only Potentate, the King of kings, and Lord of lords; who only hath immortality, dwelling in the light which no man can approach unto; whom no man hath seen, nor can see; to whom be honor and power everlasting. Amen" (1 Tim. 6:13-16).

Paul motivated Timothy by giving him one of the greatest doxologies (formal praise to God) in the Bible. It is reminiscent of 1 Timothy 1:17: "Now unto the King eternal, immortal, invisible, the only wise God, be honor and glory forever and ever. Amen."

Timothy had already been reminded of his calling and duties, but the motivation necessary to fulfill those duties would come from understanding the character of God.

That's the focus of Paul's doxology and the key to motivation for spiritual duty.

Is Your God Too Small?

The level of our commitment to Christian living and the impact of our ministry are directly related to our view of God. Translator J. B. Phillips coined the phrase "your God is too small" in his excellent book by the same name (N.Y.: Macmillan, 1961). He meant that many Christians are ineffective because their view of God is inadequate. On the other hand, a proper view of God results in a life of devotion, spiritual strength, and effective ministry. That's why Paul rehearsed the character of God as motivation for Timothy to fulfill his calling.

When people observe your life, what impression do they get of your God? Is He too small?

D. The Hindrances to Spiritual Duty

1. For Timothy

When you consider Timothy's rich spiritual heritage, his divine calling, and his effective ministry, you might wonder why he needed further motivation. But there will always be opposition to effective ministry, and Timothy's was no exception. He was young and alone in Ephesus, facing the difficult task of correcting serious problems in the church. He had to confront sin and false doctrine. Some people may have looked down on his youth. He may have lacked the peacemaking skills needed for such a task. He may have struggled with youthful lusts, which would have hindered his self-confidence. He may have lacked the ability to respond to the many theological and philosophical errors he faced.

There are indications that he may have been considering backing out of the ministry all together. In 2 Timothy Paul says, "Kindle afresh the gift of God which is in you through the laying on of my hands. For God has not given us a spirit of timidity, but of power and love and discipline. Therefore do not be ashamed of the testimony of our Lord. . . . Retain the standard of sound words which you have heard from me. . . . Continue in the things you have learned and become convinced of" (2 Tim. 1:6-8, 13; 3:14, NASB).

Timothy not only experienced opposition but also faced it alone since Paul had left Ephesus to minister in other areas. All in all he had a difficult assignment and needed encouragement to complete it.

2. For us

Whenever we take a firm stand on biblical truth we can expect opposition and attempts to discredit our ministry. It's often difficult to stand up under such pressure because we want other people to accept us. That presents a subtle temptation to compromise by keeping silent when we should speak.

E. The Strength for Spiritual Duty

Where do we find the strength to fulfill our duties in the midst of opposition or persecution? The answer: in God Himself. Paul's confidence in God's character compelled him and Timothy to minister, and our confidence in Him serves as our source of encouragement and motivation as well.

Ministering out of a sense of duty or obligation may not be adequate motivation to see us through times of severe opposition, criticism, or persecution. We need an unshakable confidence in God's sovereignty. If we understand His character and trust His promises, we will be less likely to compromise His truth. In Him we find the strength and courage we need to fulfill our ministries. In that sense we are reflections of our theology: our view of God determines how we live our lives.

Lesson

Paul illustrated that principle by giving Timothy one of the most magnificent descriptions of God's character in Scripture. It is a solemn doxology intended to remind Timothy of the nature of the God who had called, gifted, and ordained him to ministry.

The doxology is in 1 Timothy 6:15-16, but Paul gives additional insight into the nature of God in verses 13-14.

I. THE POWER OF GOD (vv. 13-14*a*)

"I command thee in the sight of God, who maketh all things alive, and before Christ Jesus, who before Pontius Pilate witnessed a good confession, that thou keep this commandment without spot, unrebukeable."

Paul commanded Timothy to fulfill the specific duty that God had called him to do. That command applies to us as well, because we all have spiritual duties to perform. In part, our motivation for fulfilling those duties comes from knowing we are serving the God who is the source of all life.

A. God Is the Creator of Life

Genesis 1:1 says, "In the beginning God created the heaven and the earth." God created everything. In fact, the Bible calls Him "Creator" (e.g., Rom. 1:25).

B. God Is the Sustainer of Life

Acts 17:28 says, "In Him we live, and move, and have our [existence]." All life is the reflection of God's power.

C. God Is the Preserver of Life

God protects and preserves the lives of those who love Him. Psalm 36:6 says, "O Lord, thou preservest man and beast." In Psalm 37:28 we read, "The Lord loveth justice, and forsaketh not his saints; they are preserved forever." Jesus said, "Are not two sparrows sold for a farthing? And one of them shall not fall on the ground without your Father. But the very hairs of your head are all numbered. Fear not, therefore; ye are of more value than many sparrows" (Matt. 10:29-31).

Because God gives, sustains, and preserves life, you can be confident as you follow God's direction, knowing that He's in control. You need not fear what men will do to you. Concern for self-preservation, reputation, or personal comfort will only distract you from effective ministry.

D. God Is the Restorer of Life

1. The principle explained

I believe the phrase "God, who maketh all things alive" (v. 13b) refers primarily to the resurrection power of God. The worst thing man can do to us is kill us, but that is not so bad. When we die we will be in the presence of God instantly, and we know He will raise our bodies from the grave. Paul said, "We are of good courage, I say, and prefer rather to be absent from the body and to be at home with the Lord" (2 Cor. 5:8, NASB).

2. The principle explored

a) Philippians 1:21-24—Paul said, "To me, to live is Christ, and to die is gain. But if I am to live on in the flesh, this will mean fruitful labor for me; and I do not know which to choose. But I am hard pressed from both directions, having the desire to depart and be with Christ, for that is very much better; yet to remain on in the flesh is more necessary for your sake" (NASB). Paul wasn't concerned about preserving his physical life. That's why he was able to devote himself fully to spiritual duty.

b) Acts 20:22-24—Paul said, "Now, behold, bound in spirit, I am on my way to Jerusalem, not knowing what will happen to me there, except that the Holy Spirit solemnly testifies to me in every city, saying that bonds and afflictions await me. But I do not consider my life of any account as dear to myself, in order that I may finish my course, and the ministry which I received from the Lord Jesus" (NASB). He wasn't intimidated by imprisonment or death, for his priorities were eternal rather than temporal.

c) 2 Corinthians 5:1-2—Paul said, "We know that if the earthly [body] which is our house is torn down, we have a [resurrection body] from God, a house not made with hands, eternal in the heavens. For indeed in this house we groan, longing to be clothed with our dwelling from heaven" (NASB).

d) Job 19:26—Job said, "Even after my skin is destroyed, yet from my flesh I shall see God" (NASB). Job understood the resurrection power of God.

e) Psalm 16:10-11—David said, "Thou wilt not leave my soul in sheol, neither wilt thou permit thine Holy One to see corruption. Thou wilt show me the path of life."

f) Daniel 12:2—Daniel recorded, "Many of those who sleep in the dust of the earth shall awake, some to everlasting life, and some to shame and everlasting contempt" (cf. John 5:28-29).

g) Hebrews 11:17, 19—"By faith Abraham, when he was tested, offered up Isaac. . . . He considered that God is able to raise men even from the dead" (NASB). Abraham was willing to sacrifice Isaac because he believed in God's resurrection power.

People who willingly sacrifice their lives for their spiritual duty are able to do so because they know God will raise them from the dead. That knowledge should give us courage as well. God may prolong your physical life, or He may allow you to lose it and then raise you from the dead. He alone determines which option is best, but in either case the final outcome is the same for those who love Christ: eternity in His presence.

3. The principle illustrated

The primary reason I believe verse 13 refers to God's resurrection power is Paul's illustration of Christ's confession before Pontius Pilate. Jesus fearlessly maintained His testimony in the face of death, and we are to follow His example.

a) The conspiracy against Christ

The Jewish people as a whole rejected the messianic claims of Christ. He was accused of being an insurrectionist who was involved in revolutionary activities aimed at overthrowing the Roman government. The religious leaders brought Him before Pilate claiming that He was a threat not only to Judaism but to the Roman political system as well.

Luke 23:2 tells us what they said: "We found this fellow perverting the nation, and forbidding to give tribute to Caesar, saying that he himself is Christ, a king." Their political accusations were untrue. Jesus did not set Himself against Rome. In fact, when asked by the Pharisees and Herodians if it was lawful to give tribute to Caesar, He said, "Render . . . unto Caesar the things which are Caesar's; and unto God, the things that are God's" (Matt. 22:21). However, their religious accusations were true: Jesus did claim to be the Messiah.

b) The confession of Christ

Jesus could have denied He was a king, but He boldly spoke the truth even though He understood the consequences His confession would bring. Luke 23:3 says, "Pilate asked him, saying, Art thou the King of the Jews? And he answered him, and said, Thou sayest it." The phrase "Thou sayest it" means "Yes, it is true. I am a king."

John 18:33-37 gives more detail about that conversation: "Then Pilate entered into the judgment hall again, and called Jesus, and said unto him, Art thou the King of the Jews? Jesus answered him, Sayest thou this thing of thyself, or did others tell it thee of me? Pilate answered, Am I a Jew? Thine own nation and the chief priests have delivered thee unto me. What hast thou done?

"Jesus answered, My kingdom is not of this world; if my kingdom were of this world, then would my servants fight, that I should not be delivered to the Jews;

69

but now is my kingdom not from here. Pilate, therefore, said unto him, Art thou a king, then? Jesus answered, Thou sayest that I am a king. To this end was I born, and for this cause came I into the world, that I should bear witness unto the truth. Everyone that is of the truth heareth my voice."

That was a noble confession, and Jesus knew it would cost Him His life. But He spoke the truth anyway. That's the point Paul made to Timothy: follow the example of Jesus, who when faced with the loss of His life still spoke the truth.

c) The confidence of Christ

Jesus never equivocated His message, even in the face of imminent danger and death, because He entrusted Himself to the One who raises the dead. His confidence in the Father's resurrection power is reflected throughout the New Testament.

(1) John 2:19—After Jesus purged the Temple, the Jewish leaders asked Him for a sign of His authority. He replied, "Destroy this temple, and in three days I will raise it up." He prophesied His resurrection as the sign of His authority (vv. 21-22).

(2) 1 Peter 2:23—Peter said of Jesus, "When he was reviled, reviled not again; when he suffered, he threatened not, but committed himself to him that judgeth righteously." Jesus didn't have to retaliate when He was mistreated because He knew He would be vindicated through His resurrection. He confessed openly His lordship, messianic identity, and sovereign authority. His confidence was in the Father, who judges all things righteously.

(3) Revelation 1:5; 3:14—Jesus is called "the faithful and true witness" because He displayed unflinching courage in the face of persecution, opposition, and temptation to compromise. He trusted in the resurrection power of God.

70

If you follow Christ's example, you can minister with the full confidence that even if you lose your life, God will restore it through resurrection. Jesus said, "He that findeth his life shall lose it; and he that loseth his life for my sake shall find it" (Matt. 10:39).

II. THE TRUTHFULNESS OF GOD (vv. 14b-15a)

"Until the appearing of our Lord Jesus Christ; which in his times he shall show."

A. The Explanation of His Promise

1. Its source

The source of that promise is God the Father. We know that because the doxology in verses 15-16 refers to "the blessed and only Potentate, the King of kings, and Lord of lords; who only hath immortality, dwelling in the light which no man can approach unto; *whom no man hath seen, nor can see*" (emphasis added). That can't refer to Jesus.

The Father determines when Christ appears on earth. Galatians 4:4 says, "When the fullness of the time was come, God sent forth his Son." And just as He sent His Son the first time, He will send His Son the second time. Jesus said, "Then shall they see the Son of man coming in the clouds, with great power and glory. . . . But of that day and that hour knoweth no man, no, not the angels who are in heaven, neither the Son, but the Father" (Mark 13:26, 32). In Acts 1:7 Jesus said to the disciples, "It is not for you to know the times or the seasons, which the Father hath put in His own power." The promise is fulfilled according to the Father's timing and planning.

Are You Anticipating Christ's Return?

God promised to send His Son to earth a second time, but we don't know when that will occur. Therefore, we must not settle into the world for a long, comfortable life but must live in anticipation of that great event.

71

Are you anticipating Christ's return? Does the thought of His imminent coming govern the way you live? It should!

2. Its meaning

The Greek word translated "appearing" (v. 14) literally means "the shining forth" of Christ. It refers to the visible, glorious display of Christ's returning to establish His kingdom on earth. The next event on God's prophetic calendar is the rapture of the church, but Paul is not referring to that in this passage. The rapture is somewhat secretive—believers ascend to meet Christ in the air, and He removes them from the world (1 Thess. 4:13-18). But the shining forth of Christ is His return in blazing glory to conclude human history as we know it and establish His kingdom on earth. At that time God will vindicate His Son and those who belong to Him.

B. The Vindication of His Son

Jesus said that at His return everyone on earth "shall see the Son of man coming in the clouds of heaven with power and great glory. And he shall send his angels with a great sound of a trumpet" (Matt. 24:30-31). Revelation 19:11-14 describes Christ returning on a white horse accompanied by angels and believers wearing white garments and riding white horses.

The Greek word translated "white" (*leukon*) in Revelation 19 includes the idea of dazzling brilliance. It is a picture of Christ and His followers returning to earth in dazzling brilliance to mount an offensive against the forces of Satan. Jesus will be vindicated and the erroneous verdict that He deserved death will be reversed.

C. The Vindication of His People

Colossians 3:4 says, "When Christ, who is our life, shall appear, then shall ye also appear with him in glory." Isn't that a great thought? We will accompany Him on His glorious return.

Right now unbelievers don't understand who Christians really are. They don't know that within us is the life of God and that we possess the Holy Spirit. They don't understand that we will live eternally with God and rule over the earth in the millennial kingdom. They don't know that our sins are forgiven and that we're new creatures in Christ. They don't know that someday our bodies will be redeemed and we'll be glorified with Christ.

Physically we look like everyone else. Indeed, "the earnest expectation of the creation waiteth for the manifestation of the sons of God. . . . Because the creation itself also shall be delivered from the bondage of corruption into the glorious liberty of the children of God" (Rom. 8:19, 21). And we "groan within ourselves, waiting for the adoption, that is, the redemption of our body" (Rom. 8:23). We're anxiously awaiting the day when we exchange our unredeemed flesh for a glorified body that is like Christ's resurrection body (Phil. 3:21).

John said, "Beloved . . . it doth not yet appear what we shall be, but we know that, when he shall appear, we shall be like him; for we shall see him as he is" (1 John 3:2). On that day we will be liberated from the incarceration of our fallen state, and our trust in Christ will be vindicated. Then the world will understand who we are.

D. The Application of His Promise

Our hope of future glory has important present applications.

1. Living in light of Christ's return

Focusing on Christ's future glory helps us keep a proper perspective on the daily events that affect our lives. James said, "You are just a vapor that appears for a little while and then vanishes away" (James 4:14, NASB). Our lives are very brief and will soon come to an end. Therefore to make your short life worthwhile, invest your time and efforts into advancing Christ's kingdom.

2. Living a holy life

John said, "When He appears, we shall be like Him, because we shall see Him just as He is. And everyone who has this hope fixed on Him purifies himself, just as He is pure" (1 John 3:2-3, NASB). The hope of sharing Christ's future kingdom should motivate us to live pure lives.

3. Being active in Christian service

Paul devoted his life to serving Christ so that he would receive a crown of righteousness. At the end of his life he said, "I have fought the good fight, I have finished the course [cf. Acts 20:24], I have kept the faith; in the future there is laid up for me the crown of righteousness, which the Lord, the righteous Judge, will award to me on that day; and not only to me, but also to all who have loved His appearing" (2 Tim. 4:7-8, NASB).

The Greek word translated "appearing" (*epiphaneia*) is the same word Paul uses in 1 Timothy 6:14 to refer to the shining forth of Christ at His second coming. Paul's anticipation of that great day motivated him to faithful service.

4. Experiencing victory through suffering

Paul said, "I reckon that the sufferings of this present time are not worthy to be compared with the glory which shall be revealed in us" (Rom. 8:18). You need not be concerned if people persecute you or even if they take your life, because the Christian hope is in the day "Jesus shall step forth out of his present invisibility" (R. C. H. Lenski, *The Interpretation of St. Paul's Epistles to the Colossians to the Thessalonians, to Timothy, to Titus* [Minneapolis: Augsburg, 1946], p. 723).

God has provided a magnificent future for us. We can't even imagine what it will be like in its fullness. But if we keep remembering the fact that He has provided for us, we can endure any persecution in this life as we do our spiritual duty. We should never waver or compromise.

5. Looking toward future evaluation and rewards

Paul said, "We must all appear before the judgment seat [winner's platform] of Christ, that each one may be recompensed for his deeds in the body, according to what he has done, whether good or bad [worthless]" (2 Cor. 5:10, NASB).

Paul also said, "To me it is a very small thing that I should be examined by you, or by any human court; in fact, I do not even examine myself. I am conscious of nothing against myself, yet I am not by this acquitted; but the one who examines me is the Lord. Therefore do not go on passing judgment before the time, but wait until the Lord comes who will both bring to light the things hidden in the darkness and disclose the motives of men's hearts; and then each man's praise will come to him from God" (1 Cor. 4:3-5, NASB).

Paul knew he would be evaluated by Christ, so he lived accordingly.

After discussing the power and truthfulness of God in verses 13-15, Paul launches into his magnificent doxology. Each phrase in the doxology expresses the incomparable greatness of God: "the blessed and only Potentate, the King of kings, and Lord of lords; who only hath immortality, dwelling in the light which no man can approach unto; whom no man hath seen, nor can see; to whom be honor and power everlasting. Amen" (vv. 15-16).

III. THE BLESSEDNESS OF GOD (v. 15b)

"Who is the blessed."

A. The Definition

The Greek word translated "blessed" (*makarios*) means "happy," "content," or "fulfilled." It is the absence of unhappiness, frustration, or anxiety concerning anyone or anything. God is perfectly content because He controls everything.

B. The Application

Quite often we experience unhappiness or frustration, yet God is perfectly content. That doesn't mean He isn't concerned about our problems. On the contrary, He cares deeply about our anxieties, but He knows their outcome. Nothing is beyond His control, and everything works out exactly as He has planned. Therefore He is totally content and happy.

Those who love Him and submit to His sovereign control over their lives can experience that same happiness and contentedness. Psalm 2:12 says, "Blessed are all they who put their trust in him." Psalm 112:1 says, "Blessed is the man who feareth the Lord, who delighteth greatly in his commandments." Psalm 128:1 says, "Blessed is every one that feareth the Lord, that walketh in his ways."

How wonderful to know that no matter what opposition or persecution comes your way, God is in control. He has emotions such as anger, wrath, love, and compassion, but they never create worry or fear in His mind because He is sovereign.

IV. THE SOVEREIGNTY OF GOD (v. 15c)

"The . . . only Potentate, the King of kings, and Lord of lords."

A. The Terms

1. "Potentate"

The Greek word translated "Potentate" (*dunastēs*) refers to God the Father and speaks of inherent power and absolute monarchy. No one else can compete with Him.

Can Satan Overpower God?

Satan is a powerful enemy; but although he tries, he can't compete with God. God is the Supreme Ruler (1 Tim. 6:15). He created Satan, exalted him, demoted him, expelled him from heaven, and sentenced him to eternal hell. Satan can never overpower God.

76

Moses said to the Israelites, "Unto thee it was shown, that thou mightest know that the Lord, he is God; there is none else beside him. . . . Know therefore this day, and consider it in thine heart, that the Lord, he is God in heaven above, and upon the earth beneath; there is none else" (Deut. 4:35, 39). God is the absolute and sovereign ruler. Satan is powerful—he bruised our Lord's heel, but He in turn crushed his head (Gen. 3:15).

2. "King of kings, and Lord of lords"

That phrase literally means "the King of those who are functioning as kings and the Lord of those who are functioning as lords." It further amplifies God's sovereignty. Some people believe Paul was referring to Christ, since He is called by that title in Revelation 17:14 and 19:16, but we have seen that Paul couldn't have had Christ in mind here (v. 16). Also, the same title is used in the Old Testament to describe the Father.

a) Deuteronomy 10:17—"The Lord your God is God of gods, and Lord of lords."

b) Psalm 136:3—"Oh, give thanks to the Lord of lords."

c) Daniel 2:47—"The king answered unto Daniel, and said, Of a truth it is that your God is the God of gods, and the Lord of kings."

B. The Rebuttal

I believe Paul's statement is a conscious rebuttal to emperor worship. At that time there was a growing cult that worshiped the Caesars in an attempt to immortalize them after their deaths. Timothy was in the Roman stronghold of Ephesus, where the citizens were expected to follow that practice. In proclaiming that God is the only sovereign authority, Paul may have been denying such practices (cf. Kenneth Wuest, *Wuest's Word Studies from the Greek New Testament: The Pastoral Epistles* [Grand Rapids: Eerdmans, 1952], p. 101).

C. The Application

1. God's sovereignty eliminates worry

   If God is the only sovereign authority, you can rest in the knowledge that no one else can ultimately control or defeat you. That is great encouragement.

2. God's sovereignty eliminates the need to manipulate people

   Knowing God is in control means you don't have to resort to manipulating people or compromising biblical truth to accomplish the goals of your ministry. For example, if I believed salvation came through man's exercising his own will apart from the sovereign election of God and that it was my responsibility to convince people to receive Christ, I couldn't handle the anxiety that would create in me. If I felt that my preaching techniques or the cleverness of my invitation were able to save people from hell, I would feel guilty about every person I couldn't convince.

   But the Bible teaches that God is sovereign and that He will graciously redeem those upon whom He has set His love. The Christian's responsibility is to proclaim God's Word faithfully, not to manipulate people.

3. God's sovereignty eliminates the need to manipulate one's circumstances

   In addition, if I thought I was responsible to make sure my life turned out right and that I could do so by controlling my circumstances, I'd be a tough guy to live with. But I believe in God's control over every aspect of my life, and all I want to do is be faithful to Him. Every time I encounter unexpected circumstances I have another opportunity to wait upon God to discover what He has in mind. That's a wonderful assurance.

   Isaiah 46:11 says, "I have spoken it, I will also bring it to pass; I have purposed it, I will also do it." God does everything He promises to do, and He said all who love Him will be "conformed to the image of his Son" (Rom.

78

8:29). People who don't trust in God's sovereignty are apt to experience worry, fear, and anxiety when things go wrong—and they will go wrong at some point, because no one is able to fully control his circumstances.

Joseph said to his brothers, "As for you, you meant evil against me, but God meant it for good" (Gen. 50:20, NASB). He had courage in the midst of difficult circumstances because He trusted in the sovereignty of God. We should do the same.

V. THE ETERNALITY OF GOD (v. 16a)

"Who only hath immortality."

A. The Definition

In the first century A.D. it was fashionable to treat dead Roman emperors as if they were immortal, but Paul affirmed that only God is immortal. That does not mean that only God will live forever. Paul meant that only God possesses inherent immortality—He alone is immortal by nature.

The Greek word translated "immortality" (*athanasia*) means "deathless." Another Greek word (*aphtharsia*) is used to speak of incorruptibility, but Paul's thought goes beyond incorruptibility to include the length of God's life: It is unending because He is incapable of death. People have immortality because God grants it to them just as He grants life itself, but He alone is inherently immortal.

B. The Documentation

The immortality of God is recorded throughout Scripture.

1. Psalm 36:9—David said, "With thee is the fountain of life." God is the source of life.

2. Isaiah 40:28—God is "the everlasting God."

3. Daniel 4:34—King Nebuchadnezzar said, "I praised and honored him who liveth forever, whose dominion is an everlasting dominion."

4. Psalm 90:1-2—The psalmist said, "Lord, thou hast been our dwelling place in all generations. Before the mountains were brought forth, or ever thou hadst formed the earth and the world, even from everlasting to everlasting, thou art God."

5. Habakkuk 1:12—Habakkuk said, "Art thou not from everlasting, O Lord, my God, mine Holy One?" He asked that question because he couldn't understand why God would use the evil Chaldeans to chasten unrepentant Israel. He saw that as a violation of God's covenant and felt that God should bring revival upon Israel rather than judgment. He restored his own perspective by reminding himself that God is eternal and therefore bigger than any event in human history—even the devastation of His own people.

It's comforting to know that God surpasses any given event in human history. He is outside of and unaffected by time, circumstances, sin, demons, or men. He is the eternal and sovereign God.

C. The Application

What a joy it is to know that the eternal God, who has planned all human history, is available to us. No matter what are our circumstances, He understands and helps us, because He is infinitely greater than any problem we have.

VI. THE HOLINESS OF GOD (v. 16b)

"Dwelling in the light which no man can approach unto; whom no man hath seen, nor can see."

A. The Explanation

1. God is holy

Paul's mention of light suggests the pure holiness of God. He is utterly separate from sin and sinners. Exodus 15:11 says, "Who is like unto thee, O Lord, among the gods? Who is like thee, glorious in holiness?" That verse associates His glory with His holiness. In 1 Samuel 2:2 Hannah says, "There is none holy like the Lord."

2. God is unapproachable

Mankind cannot approach God in His undiminished glory.

a) Psalm 104:1-2—The psalmist said, "O Lord my God, thou art very great; thou art clothed with honor and majesty, who coverest thyself with light as with a garment."

b) Exodus 33:11; 18-20—God spoke to Moses "face to face" (v. 11), but when Moses asked God to show him His glory (v. 18), God said, "Thou canst not see my face; for there shall no man see me, and live" (v. 20). Even Moses had to be sheltered from the full glory of God. Otherwise he would have died immediately.

c) Matthew 5:8—Jesus said, "Blessed are the pure in heart; for they shall see God." That vision of God involves the intimate knowledge of God that true believers have, but it's still only partial vision. Even believers can't see God in His fullness and live.

d) 1 Corinthians 13:12—Paul said, "Now we see in a mirror, darkly; but then, face to face." That is another reference to the intimate knowledge of God that the glorified believer will have, but it still falls short of the full knowledge of God's glory.

e) 1 John 3:2—John said, "We know that, when he shall appear, we shall be like him; for we shall see him as he is." That is a vision of Christ.

God the Father is unapproachable in the sense that man has never seen nor will he ever see His full glory. I believe that even in heaven we will only see a portion of it. It will certainly be a greater portion than anyone has ever seen in this world, but we won't see the full, blazing, eternal, immense glory of God.

B. The Rationale

If God is so unapproachable, why did Paul include that thought in a doxology designed to motivate Timothy to fulfill his spiritual duty? The answer is twofold.

1. To show that God never makes mistakes

It's one thing to have a sovereign God who is in control of everything, but it's another thing to have a sovereign God who always does what is right.

2. To show that God doesn't tolerate sin

God will always deal with sin. Someday He will destroy it utterly, thereby vindicating His holiness and the holiness of His people. What a great day that will be!

C. The Application

It's wonderful to know we have a sovereign, holy God. We can do what He has called us to do, confident that all our circumstances are designed by Him and that He never makes a mistake. If anyone persistently persecutes us, speaks evil against us, or in any way distracts us from the work of God's kingdom, he will one day feel His vengeance.

Conclusion

Paul's doxology appropriately ends with a refrain of praise: "To whom be honor and power everlasting. Amen" (v. 16). "Amen" means "let it be." "Honor" means respect. The Greek word translated "power" (*kratos*) means "dominion." Paul was acknowledging the praise and respect of which God is worthy.

Our God is the preserver of all life and the giver of glorious promises for the future. He is the blessed, sovereign, and eternal God of the universe. By understanding His character you can draw strength and courage to complete whatever He has called you to do. Hebrews 13:6 says, "We may boldly say, The Lord is my helper, and I will not fear what man shall do unto me." We need not fear men because we know the character of our God. That's true motivation for spiritual duty!

Focusing on the Facts

1. What was Paul's standard for spiritual duty (Acts 26:19; see p. 63)?
2. How did Paul motivate Timothy to fulfill his spiritual duty (see p. 63)?
3. What did J. B. Phillips mean by the statement, "Your God is too small" (see p. 64)?
4. What were some of the hindrances Timothy apparently faced in his ministry (see pp. 64-65)?
5. We are living reflections of our _____ (see p. 65).
6. What are four aspects of God's power (vv. 13-14; see pp. 66-67)?
7. What does Philippians 1:21-24 indicate about Paul's attitude toward spiritual duty (see p. 67)?
8. What charges were brought against Christ at his trial before Pilate (Luke 23:2; see p. 69)? Were those charges true? Explain.
9. How was Jesus able to suffer persecution without retaliating (1 Pet. 2:23; see pp. 70)?
10. How do we know that Paul's doxology in verses 15-16 refers to God the Father (see p. 71)?
11. Define "appearing" as used in verse 14 (see p. 72).
12. How will Christ's return vindicate Him (see p. 72)?
13. How will Christ's return vindicate believers (see pp. 72-73)?
14. What present application of the coming of Christ is given in 1 John 3:2-3 (see p. 74)?
15. What was Paul's conclusion after comparing the present suffering of believers with their future glory (Rom. 8:18; see p. 74)?
16. Define "blessed" as used in verse 15 (see p. 75).
17. How does the blessedness of God apply to our lives (see p. 76)?
18. Can Satan overpower God? Explain (see pp. 76-77).
19. What issue might Paul have addressed in verse 15 when he referred to God as "King of kings, and Lord of lords" (see p. 77)?
20. How does the sovereignty of God apply to our lives (see p. 78)?
21. Define "immortality" as used in verse 16 (see p. 79).
22. Paul's mention of light suggests the _____ _____ of God (see p. 80).

23. What does Paul mean in verse 16 when he says God is unapproachable (see p. 81)?
24. How does the holiness of God apply to us (see p. 82)?
25. What does the end of the doxology acknowledge (see p. 82)?

Pondering the Principles

1. We have seen that our commitment to Christian living and the impact of our ministry is directly related to our view of God. A correct view of God gives us courage and motivation to face life's challenges. An incorrect view of God can lead to uncertainty and hesitancy. A great way to develop a proper view of God is to meditate on His attributes. We have considered His power, truthfulness, blessedness, sovereignty, eternality, and holiness. Other attributes to consider are:

   • The knowledge of God—John 21:17; 1 John 3:20
   • The wisdom of God—Proverbs 8; Romans 11:33
   • The goodness of God—Psalm 145:8-9; Matthew 5:45
   • The love of God—Romans 5:8; 1 John 3:1; 4:8-10, 16
   • The grace of God—2 Corinthians 8:9; 1 Peter 5:10
   • The mercy of God—Psalm 86:5; Luke 1:50; 2 Corinthians 1:3; Ephesians 2:4; James 5:11
   • The justice of God—Psalm 89:14; Proverbs 21:3; Acts 17:31

   Select one attribute each day as a point of focus for prayer and praise, and consider how each attribute applies to your life.

2. Paul presented Jesus as the example of uncompromising integrity amidst severe persecution. Peter said He never retaliated when unjustly accused but "kept entrusting Himself to Him who judges righteously" (1 Pet. 2:22, NASB). Jesus had a spiritual duty to perform and knew He would ultimately be vindicated. Are you facing persecution for Christ's sake? Be encouraged by this reminder from Scripture: "If you are reviled for the name of Christ, you are blessed, because the Spirit of glory and of God rests upon you" (1 Pet. 4:14, NASB).

3. Do you ever wonder why a sovereign God seemingly permits evil to go unpunished? If so, you're not alone. The prophet Ha-

84

bakkuk struggled with the same question. Read Habakkuk 1:1-11 to see how he questioned God (vv. 1-4) and how God replied (vv. 5-11). Was Habakkuk's concern valid? What was God doing about the situation? Even though we don't always understand how God is working, remember that ultimately all sin will be punished (Rev. 20:11-15). Can you say with Habakkuk that no matter what the situation appears to be, you'll find your joy and strength in the Lord (Hab. 3:17-19)?

5
Handling Treasure—Part 1

Outline

Introduction

Review

Lesson
I. Handling Riches (vv. 17-19)
  A. The Objects of the Command (v. 17*a*)
    1. Rich people defined
    2. Rich people depicted
  B. The Specifics of the Command (vv. 17*b*-19)
    1. The dangers to avoid (v. 17*b-d*)
      a) Pride (v. 17*b*)
        (1) The temptation of a superior attitude
        (2) The testimony of Scripture
      b) Overconfidence (v. 17*c-d*)
        (1) The consequences
          (*a*) A certain fall
          (*b*) A selfish independence
        (2) The contrast (v. 17*d*)
          (*a*) God's gift
          (*b*) God's glory
    2. The duties to fulfill (v. 18)
      a) Doing good
      b) Being rich in good works
      c) Being generous
      d) Being willing to share personally
    3. The investment to consider (v. 19)
      a) The life to live
      b) The life to avoid

Introduction

Although the apostle Paul deals with two different subjects in 1 Timothy 6:17-21, the theme of the passage is essentially handling treasure. At one time or another, every one of us has handled something valuable that belonged to someone else. As a child you may remember your mother's asking you not to touch things in the department store. Whenever you have held something breakable, you may have feared dropping it. I remember the first time someone put a baby in my arms. I was overwhelmed by the fragile nature of such a little life. Perhaps you know what it's like to borrow someone's new car and then regret it, because you can't find a place to park where the door won't get dinged.

When we're entrusted with something of value, we assume a great responsibility. That's the matter Paul addresses in 1 Timothy 6:17-21. God has given us His riches and truth to handle. Yet we are but stewards of those gifts, not owners. Much of the Christian life is based on how we handle what God has entrusted to us.

The entire epistle of 1 Timothy is a call to spiritual duty. Paul sent Timothy to Ephesus to set that church in order. He closed the epistle with a reaffirmation and summary of Timothy's duty to the church.

Review

Paul introduces the subject of riches in 1 Timothy 6:5, where he chastises false teachers for "supposing that gain is godliness." In verses 9-10 he says, "They that will be rich fall into temptation and a snare, and into many foolish and hurtful lusts, which drown men in destruction and perdition. For the love of money is the root of all evil, which, while some coveted after, they have erred from the faith, and pierced themselves through with many sorrows." False teachers are motivated by money because they need it to indulge their lusts. From the beginning of recorded history until the day Jesus returns, they will continue to be so motivated.

Lesson

I. HANDLING RICHES (vv. 17-19)

However Paul didn't end his treatment of the subject of money with a discussion of false teachers. If he had, some might falsely accuse everyone who has money of loving it or of having gained it through ill-conceived motives. Verses 9-10 refer to the would-be rich, but verses 17-19 speak to those who are rich already—to wealthy Christians in the church. Paul calls them to a proper stewardship of their wealth. Many rich people are not motivated only to seek riches. They may have inherited their money, gained it through proficiency in their work, or obtained it through providential circumstances. It's not necessarily true that rich people love money and that poor people don't. Verses 17-19 make clear that it isn't a sin to be rich, but it is a sin to misuse one's wealth.

How Does Wealth Relate to Christians?

In a prosperous city such as Ephesus, there were obviously some wealthy members of the church. Since 1 Timothy 6:1-2 instructs both slaves and masters, we can assume that those believing masters had means that surpassed that of their servants. Most churches are likely to have their share of wealthy members—and that is by God's design.

1. Deuteronomy 8:18—"It is [God] who giveth thee power to get wealth."

2. 1 Chronicles 29:12—"Both riches and honor come [from God]."

3. 1 Samuel 2:7—"The Lord maketh poor, and maketh rich; he bringeth low, and lifteth up."

The Bible teaches that people are poor or rich because of God's design. He allows each of us to have what we have. That's why Paul said, "I have learned to be content in whatever circumstances I am" (Phil. 4:11, NASB).

Paul neither condemned the rich nor claimed that they were more blessed by God because they had money. Some people who have nothing are at the apex of God's blessing, while some who have everything are in utter misery and are rejected by God. Never equate material prosperity with God's blessing. Actually, poverty has a wonderful benefit: you don't have to make decisions about how you spend your money! That simplifies life, causes you trust in God, and makes every small gift that comes your way the source of great joy. Don't underestimate the value of having little.

A. The Objects of the Command (v. 17a)

"Charge [command] them that are rich in this age."

The Greek text is literally translated "in the now age" or "in the present age." Paul is referring to people who have treasure in this present world. They are rich in mundane things, not spiritual things. The Greek word translated "charge" means "to command." This is a command for rich people.

1. Rich people defined

Perhaps you don't consider yourself rich because you don't have a Mercedes, a Rolls Royce, a BMW, a house on a hill, a large bank account, a boat, or a camper. But "rich" in this verse means you simply have more than you need to provide your food, clothing, and shelter—the necessities of life. If you have discretionary funds, you have more than you need. Thus you are rich.

Many of you may find that by the time you've made your house payment, paid your car loans, and clothed and fed your family, you have nothing left. But most of you are still rich. Why? Because you choose to eat $15 meals when you go out instead of $4 meals. Instead of owning one suit of clothes, you have twelve. Instead of having a car that merely gets you around, you choose one that has everything. Instead of having a warm place where you can eat and sleep, you choose to live in a furniture store you call home. Those are the choices many of us have made with our discretionary dollars.

I can't tell you specifically what God wants you to do with the money He has chosen to give you. I'm not saying we should all have one-room apartments with boxes to sit on and cots to sleep on, or that we should wear the same thing all the time. I don't believe the Lord advocates that, necessarily. But scripturally we are considered rich if we have discretionary dollars to spend. I don't scrape by on a minimum amount of food. I'm not wearing threadbare clothes or living in a dingy apartment, crying to God for my next day's provision. Rather, I have the privilege of making daily decisions about how to use what God has given me. So do most of the people in our country.

2. Rich people depicted

There is nothing wrong with being rich. In Acts 16:14-15 we meet Lydia, a rich businesswoman who was able to house the apostle Paul and his traveling companions. Dorcas was a wealthy lady who was able to make garments and give them to the poor (Acts 9:36). Philemon was a wealthy man whose house was so big that a church met there (Philem. 2). There were many people like them in the Bible. The issue is not whether you have money, but what you choose to do with it.

B. The Specifics of the Command (vv. 17b-19)

Paul didn't command the rich to give all their money away and take vows of poverty. Yet we are to follow certain guidelines when dealing with our money.

1. The dangers to avoid (v. 17b-d)

a) Pride (v. 17b)

"That they be not high-minded."

The first danger relates to our attitude toward other people. Riches have a way of making us think we're better than those who have less than we do. That's a part of our fallen nature. Riches and pride are twins—the more you have, the more you tend to battle pride and self-exaltation.

(1) The temptation of a superior attitude

"High-minded" is translated from two Greek words meaning "to think in a haughty way." Rich people are constantly faced with the temptation to put on an air of superiority. Some dress in a way that flaunts their riches. Some drive certain cars to show off. And some adopt a certain lifestyle to try to convey that they're better, wiser, and more successful than everyone else.

Psalm 73:12 says, "These are the ungodly, who prosper in the world; they increase in riches." The psalmist was saying not to view prosperity as a mark of righteousness. There are many godly people who have little. I receive letters from pastors who don't have enough money to buy books—not even a new Bible. There is no correlation between righteousness and bank accounts. It is tragic that some Christians believe you are especially blessed by God if He has chosen to give you many worldly goods. Many righteous people suffer in their poverty, while many wicked people prosper.

It is difficult to be wealthy and maintain a humble spirit. There's always the temptation to stop doing things for yourself. No longer do you need to clean your house, mow your lawn, or wash your car. The more money you have, the less you tend to do. Ultimately you think you can begin treating people as servants. You're on top of the pile, dictating what everyone else should do. Once you're in that position, it's easy to come under the illusion that you gained your wealth solely because of your own ability. Proverbs 28:11 warns, "The rich man is wise in his own conceit." Proverbs 18:23 says, "The rich answereth roughly." Why? Because they can grow accustomed to using people.

In contrast, Philippians 2:3-4 says we're to be humble, not just looking to our own affairs but also to the affairs of others. That was a foreign attitude to the Ephesians, because Greek culture mocked humility and exalted pride—just as our society does today. Humility is not considered a virtue.

(2) The testimony of Scripture

(a) Ezekiel 28:2-5—"Say unto the prince of Tyre, Thus saith the Lord God: Because thine heart is lifted up, and thou hast said, I am a god, I sit in the seat of God, in the midst of the seas, yet thou art a man, and not God, though thou set thine heart as the heart of God, behold, thou art wiser than Daniel; there is no secret that they can hide from thee. With thy wisdom and with thine understanding thou hast gotten thee riches, and hast gotten gold and silver into thy treasuries; by thy great wisdom and by thy merchandise hast thou increased thy riches, and thine heart is lifted up because of thy riches." That's the soliloquy of a man who thinks he is great. The chapter eventually moves into a discussion of Satan (vv. 11-19), who affirmed the king of Tyre in his pride. Verses 2-5 reflect the typical attitude of a person enamored with his wealth.

(b) James 2:1-9—James rebuked the church for giving the best seats to the wealthy and for slighting the poor. They were violating the royal law of love. Money has a way of bringing out the worst in people.

b) Overconfidence (v. 17c-d)

(1) The consequences

"Nor trust in uncertain riches."

The Greek word translated "trust" (elpizō) could be translated "to have hope in" or "to fix one's hope on." The constant temptation for the rich is to put their hope in their money and possessions.

93

(*a*) A certain fall

    (i) Proverbs 11:28—"He that trusteth in his riches shall fall."

    (ii) Luke 12:16-21—Jesus related this parable to the disciples: "The ground of a certain rich man brought forth plentifully. And he thought within himself, saying, What shall I do, because I have no place to bestow my crops? And he said, This will I do: I will pull down my barns, and build greater; and there will I bestow all my crops and my goods. And I will say to my soul, Soul, thou hast much goods laid up for many years; take thine ease. Eat, drink, and be merry. But God said unto him, Thou fool, this night thy soul shall be required of thee; then whose shall those things be, which thou hast provided? So is he that layeth up treasure for himself, and is not rich toward God."

(*b*) A selfish independence

When you have a lot, you tend to trust in your riches, but when you have a little, you need to trust in God. One benefit of having just enough to live on is that you're totally dependent on God. When He provides, you're very grateful. I believe one reason many Christians in America are apathetic is that they don't think they need God very much. They have replaced Him with their estate planners and retirement plans. I'm not saying we should ignore those things or be foolish in handling our money. But we must be sure not to ignore the leading of the Holy Spirit when we are deciding what to do with it. It's hard for me to understand anyone's putting more trust in what they have in a bank than in the eternal God. Proverbs 23:5 says that earthly riches quickly disappear.

I'm sure there are times when you sense in your heart the need to give some money to a particular family in need, or to give to the Lord's work in some area. But often our tendency is to resist that urge, for we know that if we take anything out of our savings, it will cut down our interest and disturb our financial plans. If you ignore the Holy Spirit's leading in that area, it's because your confidence is in your wealth and not in God. That is foolish. In ancient times wealth was uncertain because wars were frequent and people were conquered by invading nations. When that happened money was very unstable. It is just as unstable today.

James 1:17 says, "Every good gift and every perfect gift is from above, and cometh down from the Father of lights." Don't trust the provision more than the Provider.

(2) The contrast (v. 17*d*)

"But in the living God, who giveth us richly all things to enjoy."

(*a*) God's gift

We are to trust in God, who possesses all things—He owns the cattle on a thousand hills (Ps. 50:10). He has bountifully given us "all things" (Gk., *plousios*). God is so good and so gracious. *Plousios* is the same word translated "pleasure" in the phrase "the pleasures of sin" (Heb. 11:25). However, in 1 Timothy 6:17 it refers to legitimate pleasure, not illicit pleasure.

Ecclesiastes 5:18-20 says, "Behold that which I have seen; it is good and fitting for one to eat and to drink, and to enjoy the good of all his labor that he taketh under the sun all the days of his life, which God giveth him; for it is his portion. Every man also to whom God hath

95

given riches and wealth, and hath given him power to eat thereof, and to take his portion, and to rejoice in his labor; this is the gift of God. For he shall not much remember the days of his life, because God answereth him in the joy of his heart." That man doesn't pine over the past—he enjoys the present because God has been so gracious.

(b) God's glory

Many people have used Ecclesiastes 5:18-20 as a justification for self-indulgence. But that clearly wasn't Solomon's intention (cf. Eccles. 2:4-11). What is the highest form of enjoyment for a Christian? It is certainly not self-indulgence, fleshly gratification, or sensual pleasure. Rather it is the joy that comes from bringing glory to the Lord.

Spiritual delight comes from a proper use of wealth and from seeing it as a gift of God. You don't own your money or your possessions—you manage them for God. He gives them to you as a test to see where your heart is. Jesus said, "Where your treasure is, there will your heart be also" (Matt. 6:21). If you lay up treasure on earth, that's where your heart is. If you lay up treasure in heaven, that's where your heart is (Matt. 6:19-20). God wants us to enjoy the things He has given us. The best way to do that is to invest them in whatever will most honor God's name. Doing that will fill your heart with the purest kind of joy. The highest joy is to be able to invest in the advancement of God's kingdom.

The dangers to avoid are clear: riches can destroy relationships through pride, because people become aloof, uncaring, unsympathetic, selfish, and indifferent; and riches can become the hope of a person's security and can nullify his response to God. Therefore, he misses the rich joy of investing in eternity.

2. The duties to fulfill (v. 18)

"That they do good, that they be rich in good works, ready to distribute [generous], willing to share."

The rich have one basic duty, but there are four aspects of that duty.

a) Doing good

The Greek word translated "do good" (*agathourgeō*) speaks of doing that which is inherently, intrinsically, and qualitatively good. We are to do noble, excellent, praiseworthy things with our money, not things that are superficial and shallow. We should do the kinds of things that are honorable to God.

First Timothy 5:8 makes clear that we're to provide for our families. Verses 3 and 16 say we're to help support widows. Verse 17 says we're to support the elders and pastors who lead us. The early church is an example to follow for meeting the needs of others. When someone in the church was in need, others sold what they had and gave to him (Acts 2:45).

b) Being rich in good works

Instead of being rich in dollars, we need to be rich in good works. Riches do not belong in the bank, endlessly compounding interest to provide for our security. We are not to assume that they guarantee our happiness in spite of misery around us. Nor are we to stockpile our riches until our children can fight each other for them. Riches are to be used to do good works.

True riches are the accumulation of noble, generous deeds. Widows who are to be supported should be known for their good works on behalf of others (1 Tim. 5:10). Titus 3:8 says, "Be careful to maintain good works. These things are good and profitable unto men."

97

Your money won't follow you to heaven, but something else will. Revelation 14:13 says, "Their works do follow them." Your money stays here, but your spiritual deeds follow you into heaven. Every time we can give, but don't, lessens the wealth laid up for us in heaven. However, sharing what we have increases our riches in heaven.

c) Being generous

The Greek word translated "ready to distribute" (*eumetadotos*) literally means "to be generous." It clarifies the kind of noble deeds we are to do. We are to give to people in need. We're to be willing to meet any need, acting toward others in the same generous way God has acted toward us.

(1) 2 Corinthians 8:2, 9—The Macedonians gave abundantly out of their deep poverty (v. 2). They were following the example of Christ, who "though he was rich, yet for your sakes he became poor, that ye through his poverty might be rich" (v. 9).

(2) Luke 6:38—Jesus said, "Give, and it shall be given unto you; good measure, pressed down, and shaken together, and running over, shall men give into your bosom." Share what you have with others, and you will reap the rewards.

(3) 1 Chronicles 29:2, 4-17—David called on the people to give to the Temple of God. He set the example by giving generously himself: "I have prepared with all my might for the house of my God the gold for things to be made of gold, and the silver for things of silver, and the bronze for things of bronze, the iron for things of iron, and wood for things of wood; onyx stones, and stones to be set, glistening stones, and of various colors, and all manner of precious stones, and marble stones in abundance. . . . even three thousand talents of gold, of the gold of Ophir, and seven thousand talents of refined silver" (vv. 2, 4).

Then David called on the people: "Who, then, is willing to consecrate his service this day unto the Lord?" (v. 5) Verses 6-9 describe how all the people came and gave. Verse 9 says that "with perfect heart they offered willingly to the Lord; and David, the king, also rejoiced with great joy."

Next we see David's response to God: "Blessed be thou, Lord God of Israel, our father, forever and ever. Thine, O Lord, is the greatness, and the power, and the glory, and the victory, and the majesty; for all that is in the heaven and in the earth is thine. Thine is the kingdom, O Lord, and thou art exalted as head above all. Both riches and honor come of thee, and thou reignest over all; and in thine hand is power and might; and in thine hand it is to make great, and to give strength unto all. Now therefore, our God, we thank thee, and praise thy glorious name. But who am I, and what are my people, that we should be able to offer so willingly after this sort? For all things come of thee, and of thine own have we given thee. For we are strangers before thee, and sojourners, as were all our fathers; our days on the earth are as a shadow, and there is none abiding. O Lord our God, all this abundance that we have prepared to build an house for thine holy name cometh of thine hand, and is all thine own. I know also, my God, that thou testest the heart" (vv. 10-17). God gave the people riches to see how they would use them. It was a test to determine where their hearts really were.

d) Being willing to share personally

The Greek word translated "willing to share" (koinōnikos) speaks of participating in fellowship. That removes the remoteness sometimes associated with giving. Rather than merely writing a check, we're to be involved in the common life of the church. Become part of an assembly of believers, and share with those who are there. Share with God's people to build God's house. Share with those in your fellowship who have needs. Share with all whose resources are limited. And especially share for the advance of the kingdom.

What is the duty of those who are wealthy? To do good. Doing good is manifested in specific, generous, and personal deeds of kindness to others.

3. The investment to consider (v. 19)

"Laying up in store for themselves a good foundation [Gk., *themelios*, "a fund"] against the time to come, that they may lay hold on eternal life."

We're to amass a good, sound fund for the future. Most people don't want to wait; they want instant gratification. Yet if we lay up treasure in heaven, we have to wait until we get to heaven to receive the dividend.

a) The life to live

When you live investing in God's future, you are really living—living in the light of eternity, not bound by the restrictions of time. If you want to put your money in a high-yield fund, invest it in eternity. You will lay hold of real life here and now as a fringe benefit. Living is not storing up your goods and saying, "Eat, drink, and be merry." First Timothy 5:6 says, "She that liveth in pleasure is dead while she liveth." What is real life? It is eternal life.

b) The life to avoid

If you "live it up" in this life and indulge yourself with your wealth, in one respect you'll be poor for eternity. But by investing in eternity in this life, you will be rich for the ages to come. In that way, you will in this life be taking hold of what has true and lasting reality.

The most important thing to live for in this life is eternity. That's why Jesus said, "Make to yourself friends by means of the money of unrighteousness, that, when it fails, they may receive you into everlasting habitations" (Luke 16:9). What does that mean? It means that we should invest our money in winning souls to Christ. They will stand on heaven's shore to greet us when we arrive, thankful because our investment resulted in their salvation. As you perform noble deeds and give generously, you are storing up treasure in a fund that pays the highest interest—eternal interest. Nor does it need to be insured or guaranteed, for God is in charge of it. And you'll enjoy its fruits forever!

Handling riches is a great responsibility. It's also a daily responsibility. We need to pray for each other that we will be wise as we seek to obey the command of 1 Timothy 6:17-19.

Focusing on the Facts

1. What responsibility does Paul discuss in 1 Timothy 6:17-21 (see p. 88)?
2. How do rich people fit into God's plan (see p. 89)?
3. In what ways can poverty be considered beneficial (see p. 90)?
4. Who can be considered rich (see pp. 90-91)?
5. What is the first danger we are to avoid? What attitude does it affect (1 Tim. 6:17; see pp. 91-92)?
6. In what way are rich people often tempted? Explain (see p. 92).
7. Why is it difficult to be wealthy and maintain a humble spirit (see pp. 92-93)?
8. What is another danger of which wealthy people should be aware (1 Tim. 6:17; see p. 93)?
9. What happens to those who don't avoid that danger (Prov. 11:28; Luke 12:16-21; see p. 94)?
10. What happens when Christians think they have no need for God (see pp. 94-95)?
11. In what should we trust (see p. 95)?
12. What ought to be the highest form of enjoyment for a Christian (see p. 96)?
13. What does it mean to "do good" (1 Tim. 6:18; see p. 97)?
14. What kind of noble deeds are Christians to do (see p. 98)?
15. What does "willing to share" mean with regard to giving (1 Tim. 6:18; see p. 99)?
16. What is the best fund in which to invest our money? Why (1 Tim. 6:19; see p. 100)?

Pondering the Principles

1. Based on this study, would you be considered rich? How would you evaluate your use of your discretionary money? Are you wise? Inconsistent? Foolish? Are you tempted to be prideful or to trust in that which God has given you? If you are tempted in either way, you need to flee that temptation. To counteract the temptation of pride, make a study of Philippians 2:1-8. Be careful to note what's required of you in verses 1-4. If your earthly possessions mean too much to you, begin cultivating the attitude of a steward. Remember that your possessions and money belong to God. Ask Him how He would like you to manage them for Him. Look to His Word for principles on how you should invest your resources to give Him glory.

2. When you are given an opportunity to share your wealth or possessions with someone, how do you usually respond? Do you give blindly to a need? Do you analyze the need first before you give to it? Do you make judgments on the worthiness of the need before you give? Do you find that you're not usually open to sharing your resources with anyone? Since God has called us to be stewards of what He has given us, we need to be ready at a moment's notice to give whatever His Spirit prompts us to give. That means you must cultivate a certain detachment from the actual gifts He has given you. But also seek wisdom from God. He wants you to be a wise steward, not a foolish one who gives to every appeal.

6
Handling Treasure—Part 2

Outline

Introduction
A. The Call to Guard the Truth
   1. Upholding the purity of the Word
   2. Fighting for the purity of the faith
     a) Preserving the right interpretation
     b) Promoting right living
B. The Responsibility of Guarding the Truth
   1. As presented in 1 Timothy
   2. As presented in 2 Timothy
   3. As presented in Titus

Review
I. Handling Riches (vv. 17-19)

Lesson
II. Handling Truth (vv. 20-21)
A. The Duty to Fulfill (v. 20*a*)
B. The Dangers to Avoid (v. 20*b*)
   1. "Profane and vain babblings"
   2. "Oppositions of knowledge falsely so called"
C. The Fact to Consider (v. 21*a*)

Conclusion

Introduction

These are Paul's final words in his first epistle to his beloved son in the faith: "O Timothy, keep [guard] that which is committed to thy trust, avoiding profane and vain babblings, and oppositions of knowledge falsely so called, which some, professing, have erred concerning the faith. Grace be with thee. Amen" (v. 20). That is a call to guard the truth of God.

What to Look for in a Church

Recently I was listening to a local Christian radio call-in program. One listener called in with this request: "I'm searching for a church. What should I look for?" The host answered, "Fellowship. That's the most important thing to look for when choosing a church." Fellowship certainly is important, but you can find sharing, caring, and fellowship in a bar. In fact, you can find fellowship in a thousand different places, so that can't be the distinctive of the church.

Others might say the most important thing to look for when selecting a church is an interesting preacher. Someone else might say that good music is paramount. Some might look for adequate parking or a comfortable setting. I think we would be amazed—and perhaps chagrined—to find what people actually look for when they are choosing a church.

The one essential to look for in a church is the way it handles the truth. What do they believe about the Bible, and what do they believe it teaches? Do they believe it is the inerrant, authoritative Word of God? If so, are they committed to living out divine truth? How a church handles the treasure of God's truth is the most important issue, for the church is the guardian of God's Word. So keep that in mind whenever you need to look for a church.

A. The Call to Guard the Truth

Psalm 138:2 says, "Thou hast magnified thy word above all thy name." Scripture is the self-revelation of God. It is the record of who He is, what He has done, what He is doing, what He will do, and what He requires. It is holy, pure, and true. The psalmist said, "My heart standeth in awe of thy word" (Ps. 119:161). God looks for a man who trembles at His Word (Isa. 66:2). The Bible is the most sacred thing you will ever touch in this world. Paul said to the Thessalonians,

"We were allowed of God to be put in trust with the gospel" (1 Thess. 2:4). Ours is a sacred trust.

1. Upholding the purity of the Word

   In 2 Corinthians 2:17 Paul says, "We are not as many, who corrupt the word of God." Many teachers adulterate the truth of God's Word. There are hucksters who use it to line their pockets and finance their indulgences. However, Paul and his companions were true to God and Christ. They spoke the truth with integrity and sincerity (v. 17). They followed the admonitions of Deuteronomy 4:2 and Revelation 22:18-19, which say not to add to or take away from the revealed Word of God.

2. Fighting for the purity of the faith

   Jude 3 is a call to vigilance: "Ye should earnestly contend for the faith which was once delivered unto the saints." The Greek word translated "earnestly contend" is *epagōnizō*. It includes the Greek word *agōn*, from which we derive the English word *agony*. *Agōn* originally referred to a stadium. The ancient Greeks referred to a stadium as a bowl because of its shape. When we go into the "bowl" to engage in spiritual warfare, our battle is for the purity of the faith. As ministers of the gospel, our Super Bowl is a fight to preserve the truth. That fight is our *raison d'etre*.

   a) Preserving the right interpretation

      I have a difficult time dealing with people who misuse Scripture. Those who do so are not making a simple error; they are perverting God's revelation. If you pervert that, then you misrepresent God Himself. You can't twist Scripture without misrepresenting God, because Scripture is His self-revelation.

   b) Promoting right living

      Guarding the truth is not only a matter of right interpretation, but also a matter of right living. God's Word is so sacred that people have given their lives to preserve it. But there are people who play fast and loose with the truth, flippantly using it for their own ends. The severest crime against God is mishandling His revelation so that people can no longer see what He is like.

Someone who says he believes the Bible, yet lives a life that violates everything it teaches, drags God's reputation down to the level of his sin. That's why Paul said, "He that is joined unto the Lord is one spirit" (1 Cor. 6:17). But when the members of Christ are joined to a prostitute, they join the Lord to that prostitute (v. 15). When you demand that other people follow God's truth while you openly violate it, you violate a sacred trust. No true minister of God misrepresents, perverts, or cheapens the Word of the living God.

B. The Responsibility of Guarding the Truth

One consistent theme throughout 1 and 2 Timothy and Titus is the sacred responsibility to live, proclaim, and guard the truth.

1. As presented in 1 Timothy

a) Chapter 1—Paul said, "As I besought thee to abide still at Ephesus, when I went into Macedonia, that thou mightest charge [command] some that they teach no other doctrine" (v. 3). Paul put Timothy in Ephesus to guard the truth against encroaching error. In verse 4 Paul says, "Neither give heed to fables and endless genealogies, which minister questions rather than godly edifying which is in faith." Paul wanted Timothy to avoid the false teaching and pseudo-intellectualism of those who desired "to be teachers of the law, understanding neither what they say, nor that about which they affirm" (v. 7).

Paul also said, "This charge I commit unto thee, son Timothy, according to the prophecies which pointed to thee, that thou by them mightest war a good warfare, holding faith, and a good conscience, which some, having put away concerning faith, have made shipwreck [of their lives]" (vv. 18-19). The "faith" is the body of Christian truth. Timothy was to uphold it.

106

b) Chapter 2—Paul said, "For this I am ordained a preacher, and an apostle (I speak the truth in Christ, and lie not)" (v. 7). That qualification ought to follow the name of every preacher: Pastor So-and-So, who preaches the truth in Christ and doesn't lie. That's what the ministry is all about. Don't tell me what degrees you have earned; just tell me that you speak the truth. How tragic it is to see school after school, seminary after seminary, and church after church abandon the truth.

c) Chapter 3—Since the sacred trust of the man of God is to guard the truth, it is fitting that of all the qualifications for an elder, only one is a skill: "Apt to teach" (v. 2). The rest of the qualifications are moral and spiritual. Guarding the truth requires the man of God to communicate it properly.

d) Chapter 4—"The Spirit speaketh expressly that, in the latter times, some shall depart from the faith" (v. 1). Instead of guarding the truth, some ministers "[give] heed to seducing spirits, and doctrines of demons, speaking lies in hypocrisy, having their conscience seared with a hot iron" (vv. 1-2). Such hypocrites don't have any conscience because it has been seared by that kind of behavior.

In contrast Paul said to Timothy, "If thou put the brethren in remembrance of these things, thou shalt be a good minister of Jesus Christ, nourished up in the words of faith and of good doctrine" (v. 6). The "words of faith" refer to Scripture. "Good doctrine" refers to the teachings of Scripture. Paul warned Timothy to be faithful in guarding the truth because demon spirits were working through lying hypocrites. Then He said, "Refuse profane and old wives' fables" (v. 7). In verse 16 Paul says, "Take heed unto thyself and unto the doctrine; continue in them." Verse 13 tells us what the priority is: "Give attendance to reading, to exhortation [applying Scripture], to doctrine [interpreting Scripture]."

e) Chapter 5—Verse 17 says, "Let the elders that rule well be counted worthy of double honor, especially they who labor in the word and doctrine." Why are they worthy of double honor? Because they guard and teach the truth.

f) Chapter 6—"These things teach and exhort. If any man teach otherwise, and consent not to wholesome words, even the words of our Lord Jesus Christ, and to the doctrine which is according to godliness, he is proud. . . . Flee these things, and follow after righteousness, godliness, faith, love, patience, meekness. Fight the good fight of faith" (vv. 2-4, 11-12). We are to fight for truth and continue fighting until Christ returns (v. 14).

In a sense we all are guardians of the truth. As Paul discussed the privilege of Israel's identity, he said, "What advantage . . . hath the Jew? Or what profit is there of circumcision? Much every way, chiefly because unto them were committed the oracles of God" (Rom. 3:1-2). God's primary gift to Israel was His Word. The church is in the same position, for He has entrusted us with the guarding and communicating of His truth.

2. As presented in 2 Timothy

a) Chapter 1—Paul said, "Hold fast the form of sound words, which thou hast heard of me. . . . That good thing which was committed unto thee keep by the Holy Spirit, who dwelleth in us" (vv. 13-14).

b) Chapter 2—"The things that thou hast heard from me among many witnesses, the same commit thou to faithful men, who shall be able to teach others also. Thou, therefore, endure hardness, as a good soldier of Jesus Christ" (vv. 2-3). We contend in a spiritual Super Bowl. It's an ongoing battle, because God's Word is always under attack.

In verse 15 Paul says, "Study to show thyself approved unto God, a workman that needeth not to be ashamed, rightly dividing the word of truth." The Greek word translated "rightly dividing" means "cutting it straight." It was used to describe cutting a pattern, as a dressmaker cuts material according to a

108

pattern and sews the pieces together. Paul was saying that when you teach a passage of Scripture, be sure to get it right. Otherwise, when you put all the pieces together, they won't match. You can't be a theologian unless you're an exegete—if you don't cut the individual passages right, your theology won't match. Be an interpreter and an expositor. Understand the Word of God. Verses 16-17 say, "Shun profane and vain babblings; for they will increase unto more ungodliness. And their word will eat as doth a gangrene."

c) Chapter 3—"Evil men and seducers shall become worse and worse, deceiving, and being deceived. But continue thou in the things which thou hast learned and hast been assured of" (vv. 13-14). The guardian of Scripture knows it is "given by inspiration of God, and . . . profitable for doctrine, for reproof, for correction, for instruction in righteousness, that the man of God may be perfect [complete], thoroughly furnished unto all good works" (vv. 15-17).

d) Chapter 4—Paul says, "I charge thee, therefore, before God, and the Lord Jesus Christ, who shall judge the living and the dead at his appearing and his kingdom: preach the word; be diligent in season, out of season, reprove, rebuke, exhort with all long-suffering and doctrine. For the time will come when they will not endure sound doctrine but, after their own lusts, shall they heap to themselves teachers, having itching ears; and they shall turn away their ears from the truth, and shall be turned unto fables. But watch thou in all things, endure afflictions, do the work of an evangelist, make full proof of thy ministry" (vv. 1-5).

Paul never let go of the truth. In verse 7 he says, "I have fought a good fight, I have finished my course, I have kept the faith." That's the attitude you ought to have at the end of your life. When I reach the end of my life, the question God asks won't be what was the size of my church, how successful was my ministry, how many radio stations broadcast my program, or how many books did I write. The crucial question will be, did I handle the truth correctly? Paul said to the

Corinthians, "It is required in stewards, that a man be found faithful" (1 Cor. 4:2).

3. As presented in Titus

a) Chapter 1—An elder is to be "holding fast the faithful word as he hath been taught, that he may be able by sound doctrine both to exhort and to confute the opposers. For there are many unruly and vain talkers and deceivers . . . whose mouths must be stopped, who subvert whole houses, teaching things which they ought not, for filthy lucre's sake" (vv. 9-11).

b) Chapter 2—Paul said, "Speak thou the things which become sound doctrine . . . in all things showing thyself a pattern of good works; in doctrine showing uncorruptness, gravity, sincerity, sound speech, that cannot be condemned . . . not purloining, but showing all good fidelity [integrity], that they may adorn the doctrine of God, our Savior, in all things" (vv. 1, 7-8, 10).

c) Chapter 3—"Avoid foolish questions, and genealogies, and contentions, and strivings about the law; for they are unprofitable and vain. A man that is an heretic, after the first and second admonition, reject, knowing that he that is such is subverted, and sinneth, being condemned of himself" (vv. 9-11).

In 1 Timothy, 2 Timothy, and Titus, Paul instructs all ministers to uphold the truth of God.

Review

I. HANDLING RICHES (vv. 17-19; see pp. 89-101)

Lesson

II. HANDLING TRUTH (vv. 20-21)

A. The Duty to Fulfill (v. 20a)

"O Timothy, keep [guard] that which is committed to thy trust."

The Greek word translated "guard" (*phulassō*) is used to refer to valuables kept in a safe place. The phrase translated "that which is committed to thy trust" is just one word in Greek—*parathēkē*, meaning "the deposit." Timothy was to guard the deposit, which is the truth of God. By saying, "O Timothy," Paul was pleading with him to guard what had been deposited with him as a sacred trust.

The Christian message is not the minister's own creation. It isn't something he is entitled to embellish. It is a divine trust that cannot be diminished or increased without serious consequence.

B. The Dangers to Avoid (v. 20b)

1. "Profane and vain babblings"

   The Greek word translated "profane" (*bebelos*) originally was used to refer to everything outside the sacred grounds of a temple. It then came to mean anything that was not sacred. All pseudo-intellectual musings, neo-orthodox theories, and private interpretations that attack Scripture are profane. They have no connection with God, His truth, or His holiness. The Greek word translated "avoid" means "to go out of the way" or "to turn aside from." The tense implies that we're to continually steer clear of such things.

   God's man is to guard the truth and stay away from error. The Greek word translated "babblings" refers to empty utterances, useless arguments, and meaningless talk unrelated to truth.

111

2. "Oppositions of knowledge falsely so called"

The Greek word translated "oppositions" (*antithesis*) is a technical term used in rhetoric for a counter-proposition in a debate. Those who refute Scripture have an unsound base of knowledge. Paul warned Timothy to stay away from anything claiming to be the truth that really wasn't.

C. The Fact to Consider (v. 21*a*)

"Which some, professing, have erred concerning the faith."

Some of the people who were proclaiming things contrary to the truth had deviated from the faith. Therefore they had abandoned their sacred trust. Such people lead many others with them. Peter said, "Many shall follow their pernicious ways" (2 Pet. 2:2).

Conclusion

What is the church? It is primarily a depository of God's truth. What should you look for in a church? Find out what they believe about Scripture. Ask yourself, how do they handle the treasure of God's Word?

Paul closed his epistle with a simple reminder: guard the truth (v. 20). Then he said, "Grace be with thee" (v. 21). Paul knew Timothy couldn't accomplish that awesome task unless he was given the grace of God. The Greek word for "thee" is plural. Many others besides Timothy would benefit from his letter, so Paul embraced the whole church in that statement. We all have a responsibility to be guardians of the truth and spiritually responsible.

How to Respond to God's Word

Before anyone can respond to God's Word, he has to believe it. God said, "This is my beloved Son, in whom I am well pleased; hear ye him" (Matt. 17:5).

1. Honor it—Job said God's Word was more important to him than his necessary food (Job 23:12).

2. Study it—"Study to show thyself approved unto God" (2 Tim. 2:15).

3. Obey it—In John 8:31 Jesus says, "If ye continue in my word, then are ye my disciples indeed."

4. Love it—The psalmist exclaimed, "O, how love I thy law!" (Ps. 119:97). David said it is "sweeter also than honey and the honeycomb" (Ps. 19:10).

5. Proclaim it—I tend to remember best what I teach and preach to others. You keep what you give away. One of the best ways to guard the truth is to teach it to others. After you've poured over it in your mind and heart and have taught it to someone else, you solidify your own understanding.

We all have a sacred trust just like Timothy. We are in a war and we must stand for the truth. God commands us to do that so that we might pass on the pure, unadulterated truth to the next generation.

Focusing on the Facts

1. What should you look for when choosing a church (see p. 104)?
2. Scripture is the _____ of God (see p. 104).
3. According to 2 Corinthians 2:17, why were Paul and his companions different from other teachers (see p. 105)?
4. What is Jude 3 a call to? Explain (see p. 105).
5. What happens when someone misuses Scripture (see p. 105)?
6. If someone claims to believe the Bible yet lives a life that violates its teaching, what does that do (see p. 106)?
7. List some of the things Paul teaches in 1 Timothy about guarding the truth (see pp. 106-8).
8. What does Paul teach in 2 Timothy about guarding the truth (see pp. 108-9)?
9. What are some of the things Paul teaches in Titus about guarding the truth (see p. 110)?
10. What duty was Timothy to fulfill (1 Tim. 6:20; see p. 111)?

11. What dangers was Timothy to avoid (1 Tim. 6:20; see pp. 111-12)?
12. What happens to people who proclaim things contrary to the faith (1 Tim. 6:21; see p. 112)?
13. What did Timothy need to help him accomplish his task (1 Tim. 6:21; see p. 112)?
14. How should you respond to God's Word (see pp. 112-13)?

Pondering the Principles

1. What do you look for in a church? What was the basis of your choosing your present church? After this study, can you conclude that your church is committed to teaching and guarding the Word of God? Now evaluate your own commitment. Even if you're not a leader in your church, you still can be instrumental in preserving the purity and holiness of God's Word. Begin today to uphold God's Word by living in obedience to it.

2. Review the section on how to respond to God's Word (see pp. 112-13). On a scale of 1 to 10 how would you rate your effectiveness in each of those areas? What are your strengths? What are your weaknesses? This week take your weakest area and begin to devote yourself to God's Word in that area. An important way to cultivate each of those responses is to be sure you are reading the Bible every day. As you consistently spend time with God and His Word, your attitudes and responses will continue to improve.

7
Judgment on the Wicked Rich—Part 1

Outline

Introduction
A. A Test of One's Attitude About Money
B. A Pronouncement of Judgment on Wicked Rich People
   1. By James
      a) The perversion of wealth
      b) The possession of wealth
   2. By the prophets
C. A Letter to the Unsaved in the Church
   1. Christ's reaction
      a) In the parable of the soils
         (1) The rocky soil
         (2) The weedy soil
      b) To the rich young ruler
   2. The people's life-style

Lesson
I. The Pronouncement of Judgment (v. 1a)
   A. The Subjects of Judgment
   B. The Responses to Judgment
      1. Defining the response
         a) Weeping
         b) Howling
      2. Calling for the response
II. The Reasons for Judgment (vv. 2-6a)
   A. Useless Hoarding (vv. 2-3)
      1. A delineation of proper investments
      2. A depiction of hoarding
         a) Spoiled food
            (1) The stockpile
            (2) The corruption

    b) Moth-eaten garments
    c) Rusted money
3. A description of rust
    a) It testifies to ungodliness
    b) It functions as an executioner
4. A disregard for redemptive history
    a) The implications
       (1) A wasted life
       (2) A worthwhile life

Introduction

James 5:1-6 says, "Come now, ye rich men, weep and howl for your miseries that shall come upon you. Your riches are corrupted and your garments are moth-eaten. Your gold and silver are rusted, and the rust of them shall be a witness against you, and shall eat your flesh as it were fire. Ye have heaped treasure together for the last days. Behold, the hire of the laborers who have reaped down your fields, which is of you kept back by fraud, crieth; and the cries of them who have reaped are entered into the ears of the Lord of Sabaoth. Ye have lived in pleasure on the earth, and been wanton; ye have nourished your hearts, as in a day of slaughter. Ye have condemned and killed the just; and he doth not resist you."

The epistle of James presents several tests of living faith. James wrote to a group of Jewish Christians in a local assembly and called them to evaluate the validity of their faith. He knew that wherever there is wheat, the devil sows tares (Matt. 13:24-30, 36-43). He didn't want anyone to be under the illusion that he was a Christian when he really wasn't.

A. A Test of One's Attitude About Money

A person's attitude toward wealth reveals his spiritual state. This particular passage is aimed at those who claim to love God, yet obviously love money. Their life is totally controlled and governed by that love. Thus, their spiritual state is revealed by their relationship to riches. James did not invent this test; he was echoing a test our Lord originated.

116

1. Matthew 6:19-21—"Lay not up for yourselves treasures upon earth, where moth and rust doth corrupt, and where thieves break through and steal, but lay up for yourselves treasures in heaven, where neither moth nor rust doth corrupt, and where thieves do not break through nor steal; for where your treasure is, there will your heart be also." Jesus knows where your heart is simply by looking at where you put your treasure.

2. Luke 16:11-14—"If, therefore, ye have not been faithful in the unrighteous money, who will commit to your trust the true riches?" (v. 11). Do you think God will commit the realities of His eternal kingdom to you if you haven't demonstrated an aptitude for the proper handling of money? He won't give you what is valuable if you can't handle that which is not. Verse 12 says, "If ye have not been faithful in that which is another man's, who shall give you that which is your own?" If you can't be faithful in managing God's money, why should He give you gifts of a spiritual nature to possess as your own? Jesus said, "No servant can serve two masters; for either he will hate the one, and love the other; or else he will hold to the one, and despise the other. Ye cannot serve God and money. And the Pharisees also, who were covetous, heard all these things; and they derided him" (vv. 13-14).

James based his indictment throughout his epistle on our Lord's teaching. In fact, there are many parallels in the epistle of James to the Sermon on the Mount (e.g., Matt. 6:19-21).

B. A Pronouncement of Judgment on Wicked Rich People

1. By James

James 5:1-6 is perhaps the strongest passage in the epistle. It's a pronouncement of damnation against rich people who profess faith in Christ but whose real god is money.

a) The perversion of wealth

This is a blistering, condemning, scathing diatribe against those who had perverted the wealth God gave

117

them. They had prostituted the goodness of God, who gives us the power to get wealth (Deut. 8:18), and the blessing of God, which brings us wealth (Prov. 10:22).

b) The possession of wealth

Wealth in and of itself is not sinful. By no means is it wrong to enjoy the blessings God has granted you. He has given some the stewardship of great wealth. Most of us have at least some wealth to manage—the amount varies from one person to another by God's design. While it's not wrong to possess wealth, it is wrong to misuse it. The more you have, the greater the potential for prostituting its proper use. When the love of money controls you and perverts your heart, that leads to all kinds of evil (1 Tim. 6:10). Eventually it leads to judgment by God Himself.

2. By the prophets

James spoke like the Old Testament prophets, drawing from their rich legacy of confronting greed and injustice.

a) Isaiah 3:14-15—"The Lord will enter into judgment with the ancients of his people, and their princes; for ye have eaten up the vineyard; the spoil of the poor is in your houses. What mean ye that ye beat my people to pieces, and grind the faces of the poor? saith the Lord God of hosts." The leaders of the people abused the poor for their own purposes.

b) Isaiah 10:1-4—"Woe unto them who decree unrighteous decrees, and who write grievousness, which they have prescribed, to turn aside the needy from justice, and to take away the right from the poor of my people, that widows may be their prey, and that they may rob the fatherless! And what will ye do in the day of visitation, and in the desolation which shall come from far? To whom will ye flee for help? And where will ye leave your glory? Without me they shall bow down under the prisoners, and they shall fall under the slain. For all this his anger is not turned away, but his hand is stretched out still."

c) Amos 4:1-3—"Hear this word, ye cows of Bashan, that are in the mountain of Samaria, who oppress the poor, who crush the needy, who say to their masters, Bring, and let us drink: The Lord God hath sworn by his holiness that, lo, the days shall come upon you, that he will take you away with hooks, and your posterity with fishhooks. And ye shall go out at the breaches, every cow at that which is before her, and ye shall cast them into the palace, saith the Lord."

d) Amos 8:4-10—"Hear this, O ye that swallow up the needy, even to make the poor of the land to fail, saying, When will the new moon be gone, that we may sell grain? And the sabbath, that we may set forth wheat, making the ephah small, and the shekel great, and falsifying the balances by deceit? That we may buy the poor for silver, and the needy for a pair of shoes; yea, and sell the refuse of the wheat? The Lord hath sworn by the excellency of Jacob: Surely I will never forget any of their works. Shall not the land tremble for this, and every one mourn that dwelleth in it? And it shall rise up wholly like the river; and it shall be cast out and drowned, as by the river of Egypt. And it shall come to pass in that day, saith the Lord God, that I will cause the sun to go down at noon, and I will darken the earth in the clear day; and I will turn your feasts into mourning, and all your songs into lamentation; and I will bring up sackcloth upon all loins, and baldness upon every head; and I will make it like the mourning for an only son, and the end of it like a bitter day."

Micah 2:1-5 and Malachi 3:5-11 are other diatribes against wicked rich people. In James 5:1-6 we see the author's Jewish roots revealed as he echoes the cries of the prophets.

C. A Letter to the Unsaved in the Church

James wrote his epistle to local congregations assembled in the name of Christ. Some of the members were not true Christians. That's why James presented a series of tests. Some people argue that James was not talking to people in the church. But if that were the case, why did he talk to

119

them using the second person? That he did so indicates he was writing to people in the church who would read his letter or hear it read. It would have been pointless for him to give instruction to outsiders or people who had no affiliation with or interest in the church. The direct approach assumes their presence in the church. So James was writing to people who wanted to be identified with God and Christ but refused to do so on His terms.

1. Christ's reaction

    a) In the parable of the soils

        (1) The rocky soil

        In Matthew 13:5-6 He refers to rocky soil: on the top it is soft and fertile, but underneath it is rock bed. Initially the roots from the seed flourish in the fertile ground, and the plant comes up. However, the roots eventually reach the rock bed and can't penetrate it to get enough water. So when the sun comes out, the plant burns up and dies. Jesus compared the rocky soil to the person who "heareth the word, and immediately with joy receiveth it; yet hath he not root in himself, but endureth for a while; for when tribulation or persecution ariseth because of the word, immediately he is offended" (vv. 20-21).

        (2) The weedy soil

        In verse 7 Jesus refers to soil that is full of weeds. Although a good plant grows initially, the weeds choke it out. In verse 22 Jesus says, "He . . . that received seed among the thorns [weeds] is he that heareth the word; and the care of this age, and the deceitfulness of riches, choke the word, and he becometh unfruitful." Sometimes people hear the Word, want to identify with the church, and want the promises of salvation, but they end up being preoccupied with worldly things. Although they may name the name of Christ, they don't know Him as long as their hearts are not toward God and heaven.

120

In the parables of the pearl of great price and the hidden treasure (Matt. 13:44-46), the men who wanted to buy the pearl and the field containing the treasure sold all they had in order to do so. But the people to whom James referred weren't willing to give up anything. They clung to their selfish materialistic practices, using Jesus as a front.

b) To the rich young ruler

In Matthew 19:21-22 Jesus says, "Sell what thou hast, and give to the poor, and thou shalt have treasure in heaven; and come and follow me. But when the young man heard that saying, he went away sorrowful; for he had great possessions."

2. The people's life-style

Today many people are under the illusion that they are Christians because they talk about Jesus. But their life-style betrays the fact that their real god is money and wealth. Their treasure is on earth, and that's where their heart is. Since they serve money, they can't serve God.

a) James 4:4—"Know ye not that the friendship of the world is enmity with God? Whosoever, therefore, will be a friend of the world is the enemy of God."

b) 1 John 2:15—"Love not the world, neither the things that are in the world. If any man love the world, the love of the Father is not in him."

James directed his denunciation at the rich phonies in the church. The church needs to speak to those people. We don't want them to be deceived into thinking they're Christians when their lives reveal they are consumed with the love of money. At the same time James's instruction speaks to every Christian because it reminds us of sins we must avoid.

Lesson

I. THE PRONOUNCEMENT OF JUDGMENT (v. 1a)

"Come now, ye rich men, weep and howl for your miseries that shall come upon you."

James began his denunciation with a call for wicked rich people to respond appropriately. This is the second time James used the Greek phrase translated "come now." First he used it to refer to a group of people who lived without thought for God (James 4:13). The phrase could be translated "now listen," "get this," or "see here." It's an attention-grabber in the style of Old Testament prophets.

A. The Subjects of Judgment

The group James denounced are "rich men." The context reveals that they weren't just any rich men—they had acted wickedly with their material wealth. Who are the wealthy of the world? Anyone who has more than he needs, as we have discussed previously (see pp. 90-91). If you have just enough to survive, then you have little need for discretion with your money—your expenses will force you to use it all to meet your needs. But if you have any discretionary money, you fall into the category of the rich.

B. The Responses to Judgment

1. Defining the response

James told the rich men to "weep and howl."

a) Weeping

The Greek word translated "weep" (klaiō) means "to sob out loud" or "to weep in a lamenting manner." It refers to the practice of wailing for the dead (Luke 7:13, 32; John 11:31-33) and the grief resulting from shame and regret (Matt. 26:75). In this chapter it refers to the strong emotional outbursts of those facing the inescapable judgment of hell. James used the same word in chapter 4: "Be afflicted, and mourn, and

122

weep" (v. 9). There it refers to the sorrow accompanying repentance.

b) Howling

In James 5:1 there is no call for repentance. Anyone who faces God and confesses sin laments over that sin. But the lament ends there, because where there is a lament of repentance, there is the grace of forgiveness. But no grace is seen for the wicked rich—their lament becomes a "howl." The Greek word translated "howl" (*ololuzō*) means "to shriek" or "to scream." It represents violent, uncontrollable grief.

2. Calling for the response

James 5:1 tells us why such a frantic response of overwhelming grief is appropriate: "For your miseries that shall come upon you." The Greek word translated "miseries" is used only here and in Romans 3:16. It refers to overwhelming trouble, suffering, and distress. "Your miseries" personalizes it. Those miseries will come upon every unrepentant rich person. James doesn't say when they will experience the miseries, but elsewhere in Scripture we learn it will happen at the coming of Christ. Their miseries will begin when they meet God. Judgment is inevitable. What did they do to deserve that punishment?

II. THE REASONS FOR JUDGMENT (vv. 2-6*a*)

A. Useless Hoarding (vv. 2-3)

"Your riches are corrupted and your garments are motheaten. Your gold and silver are rusted, and the rust of them shall be a witness against you, and shall eat your flesh as it were fire. Ye have heaped treasure together for the last days."

James mentions their sin in verse 3: "Ye have heaped [hoarded] treasure." The Greek verb translated "ye have heaped treasure together" is the word from which we get *thesaurus*. Those rich people hoarded treasure—they stockpiled their wealth. That was wrong because they failed to make good use of it. They piled it up uselessly. That's also a tragic sin of our own time.

1. A delineation of proper investments

When God prospers us and gives us more than we need, He does so in order that we might use our blessings properly—for His glory and to advance His kingdom. I want to leave this world just when the money God has given me runs out. I want to be sure I'm not hoarding it against some nebulous tomorrow that may never come. Instead God wants me to invest all I have in His eternal kingdom right now.

a) Providing for our families

God provides for us so we might provide for our families. The one who doesn't do that is worse than an unbeliever (1 Tim. 5:8). We are to take care of our own families and those in our extended families, especially any widows (v. 16). Beyond that, the rest of the money God has given us is to be used expressly for His glory.

b) Serving God

In the Old Testament we read that the people gave to the Temple and the Tabernacle. They gave tithes (required giving) and many freewill offerings.

(1) Luke 6:38—Jesus said, "Give, and it shall be given unto you; good measure, pressed down, and shaken together, and running over, shall men give into your bosom."

(2) 1 Corinthians 16:2—Paul said, "Upon the first day of the week let every one of you lay by him in store, as God hath prospered him."

Our wealth is to be given to the expansion and extension of the kingdom. It is not to be a legalistic enterprise; we give because our hearts are consumed with the mission of the kingdom and with love for the Lord.

c) Winning the lost

In Luke 16:9 Jesus says, "Make to yourselves friends by means of the money of unrighteousness, that, when it fails, they may receive you into everlasting habitations." You ought to use your money to make friends who will greet you in heaven when you arrive. Use your money to win people to Christ. Hoarding it uselessly violates God's intention for its use.

d) Caring for the needy

Some of the strongest words in the Old Testament are reserved for wicked people who defrauded poor people, orphans, and widows. In addition, the apostle John said, "Whosoever hath this world's good, and seeth his brother have need, and shutteth up his compassions from him, how dwelleth the love of God in him?" (1 John 3:17). Paul also mentioned the importance of remembering the poor and said he was diligent to do just that (Gal. 2:10).

e) Supporting those who minister

First Timothy 5:17-18 says, "Let the elders that rule well be counted worthy of double honor, especially they who labor in the word and doctrine. Thou shalt not muzzle the ox that treadeth out the grain; and, The laborer is worthy of his reward."

God has probably given you wealth; use it to care for your family, serve Him, win the lost, care for those in need, and support those in ministry. But don't hoard it. If you hoard your wealth, James says you'll be damned, because your heart is set on earthly things and money is your god. Anyone who stashes away money without regard for God's Word can't be a true child of God.

2. A depiction of hoarding

Apart from land and houses, the most common way of acquiring wealth in ancient times was to stockpile food, clothing, and coins.

a) Spoiled food

James 5:2 says, "Your riches are corrupted." "Riches" generally referred to food that could be stored, such as grain, wheat, barley, and perhaps dried meat. The Greek word translated "corrupted" can also be translated "decay." That makes it all the more probable that "riches" referred to food, which can easily rot.

(1) The stockpile

In James's day many people's wealth was tied up in their stockpile of grain, as in the case of the rich fool whose barns were full (Luke 12:17). That man even decided to pull his barns down and build bigger barns (v. 18). The practice of stockpiling grain was typical. People hoped to live off their stockpiles for the rest of their lives.

The Greek word translated "riches" (*ploutos*) is the name of one of the ancient Greek gods. Mythology tells us that Plutus was the son of Demeter, the goddess of the earth. His name refers to the abundant yielding of the earth. Therefore *ploutos* often referred to vegetables, grain, and meat.

(2) The corruption

James says their riches were "corrupted" (Gk., *sesēpen*, "rotted"). The noun form of that verb speaks of a putrefying sore; thus it speaks of corrupting decay. That's the reality behind stockpiling perishable goods—they won't last forever. If you hoard too much for too long, it won't be any good to anyone.

b) Moth-eaten garments

James 5:2 concludes, "Your garments are moth-eaten." The Greek word translated "garment" (*himatia*) refers to a loose outer robe, which the people often decorated with rich embroidery and jewelry. Those robes were passed on as heirlooms. When they were

126

folded and stored, the larva of moths could ruin them, just as our Lord implied (Matt. 6:19).

c) Rusted money

James 5:3 says, "Your gold and silver are rusted." The coinage of James's day was like that to which Christ referred in Matthew 6:20: "Lay up for yourselves treasures in heaven, where neither moth nor rust doth corrupt." Apparently coins in those days were not made of pure silver or gold, but were mixed with an alloy that tended to rust. So money stashed over a long period of time could easily become useless (v. 3). Then the hoarder was left with nothing.

James's point is basic: it is sinful and foolish to hoard food, clothing, and coins when all they do is rot. But even if those things remained uncorrupted, people don't. This story illustrates the point: " 'What an unfortunate wretch I am!' complained a miser to his neighbor. 'Last night someone took away the treasure which I buried in the garden, and laid a . . . stone in its place.' 'And yet you have never used your treasure,' answered his neighbor. 'Only bring yourself to believe that the stone is still your treasure, and you are none the poorer.' 'If I am none the poorer,' returned the miser, 'is not someone else the richer? The thought is enough to drive me mad' " (Spiros Zodhiates, *The Patience of Hope: An Exposition of James 4:13–5:20* [Chattanooga, Tenn.: AMG Publishers, 1981], p. 45).

Don't be irresponsible with your wealth. Don't hoard it. Don't let it corrupt you. It's been well said that if money talks, it only says good-bye. So before it can say good-bye, why not use it for God's glory?

3. A description of rust

a) It testifies to ungodliness

In verse 3 James says, "The rust of them shall be a witness against you." When people who have misused their wealth face God, the rust of their treasure will testify to their ungodliness. The ruin of the things

127

they have hoarded is a graphic picture of their own ruin. Their rotted, moth-eaten, rusted riches give loud testimony to the state of their heart. At the divine court the rusted possessions serve as inarguable evidence against those who have been covetous, selfish, and devoid of compassion.

b) It functions as an executioner

James says that rust "shall eat your flesh as it were fire" (v. 3). Rust normally corrodes slowly, but here it acts like fire—the fastest consumer of all. In the day of judgment the rust of hoarded goods will testify against the wicked rich and become a fire that consumes them. The Greek word translated "flesh" is plural. James uses the plural to mean that all wicked rich people will be executed by their own riches.

Don't forget that hell is a physical place. The flesh of the wicked will literally burn there. According to John 5:29, every evildoer will have a resurrected body suited to bear the punishment of an eternal hell and feel the flame of fire forever. Hell is reserved for those who, among others, hoard their treasure.

4. A disregard for redemptive history

James closes verse 3 by saying, "Ye have heaped treasure together [in] the last days." They lived without regard for redemptive history. They stockpiled their wealth in the messianic period. The "last days" refers to the period between the first coming of Christ and His second coming. John said, "Little children, it is the last time" (1 John 2:18). We live in the last days.

a) The implications

(1) A wasted life

Those who hoard their wealth with no regard for God's clock waste their life and their resources. If people who claim they represent Jesus Christ were really concerned about lost people going to hell and about reaching the world for Jesus Christ, they would not spend a fortune to pad their own life-styles. One who has the heart of Jesus reaches out with what he has to people in need.

(2) A worthwhile life

To live in light of the second coming is to hold loosely the wealth God gives you. Make sure you're using your wealth for His glory. If your Christianity has been an illusion and you realize that your god is money, then commit yourself to Christ before it's too late. If you're a Christian and you find yourself sinning in this area, ask God's Spirit to root your love of money out of your life. Loosen your grip on the things of this world. Develop a heart like that of the prophets, who saw all things as useful for the glory of God. God gives us new things every day. The ground replenishes our food every season. We don't need to hoard against an unknown future. But we do need to invest in the eternal kingdom, knowing that God has promised never to allow His people to be in want if they're faithful to Him.

Focusing on the Facts

1. What test of faith did James borrow from Christ? Explain the test (see pp. 116-17).
2. Toward whom is the denunciation in James 5:1-6 directed (see p. 117)?
3. How does James's denunciation echo that of the prophets (see pp. 118-19)?
4. What evidence is there that James 5:1-6 is addressed to people in the church (see pp. 119-20)?
5. How did Jesus characterize people who showed only an external commitment to Him (Matt. 13:5-7, 20-22; see p. 120)?
6. Who are the wealthy in the world (see p. 122)?
7. What two things did James tell the wicked rich people to do? Explain (James 5:1; see p. 122).
8. Why did James tell them to respond in such a way (James 5:1; see pp. 122-23)?

9. According to James 5:3, what sin did they commit (see pp. 123-24)?
10. Why does God prosper people (see p. 124)?
11. What kind of investments does God want His people to make? Explain each (see pp. 124-25).
12. How was wealth accumulated in James's day? Explain what happens to those things when they are hoarded (James 5:2; see pp. 125-27).
13. In what way is rust a witness against the wicked rich (see pp. 127-28)?
14. How does this particular rust act differently (James 5:3; see pp. 127-28)?
15. What did James mean when he said, "Ye have heaped treasure together [in] the last days" (James 5:3; see pp. 128-29?

Pondering the Principles

1. Do some serious self-examination. James 5:1-6 is directed at people in the church who were obsessed with money and possessions. To what degree do you exhibit that kind of obsession? Be honest in your evaluation. In reality are money and possessions more important to you than things of the Lord? Ask God to search your heart. If you have any doubts about your salvation, ask God to confirm that you are saved or make clear the fact that you aren't. If you are not a believer, bow before Christ right now and ask Him to be your Lord and Savior. Those of you who are convinced of your salvation yet have been disobedient in your handling of money, confess your sin to God. Make it your goal today to use what God has given you to glorify Him.

2. Are you making proper investment of the money and possessions with which God has blessed you? Are you providing for the needs of your family? In what specific ways are you using your wealth to serve God? How are you using your wealth to win people to Christ? Give some recent examples of how you helped care for people in need. In what ways do you support those people who minister to you? Those are difficult questions to answer when we aren't using our resources as God wants. To begin giving more of your wealth to God's program, you'll need to spend less on yourself. The next time you find yourself wanting to purchase something solely for yourself, don't buy it. Instead, use that money to advance God's kingdom.

8

Judgment on the Wicked Rich—Part 2

Outline

Introduction
A. The Character of the Wicked Rich
B. The Character of False Teachers
   1. As described in 2 Peter 2
   2. As described in Jude

Review
I. The Pronouncement of Judgment (v. 1)
  A. The Subjects of Judgment
  B. The Responses to Judgment
   1. Defining the response
   2. Calling for the response
II. The Reasons for Judgment (vv. 2-6a)
  A. Useless Hoarding (vv. 2-3)
   1. A delineation of proper investments
   2. A depiction of hoarding
   3. A description of rust
   4. A disregard for redemptive history
    a) The implications

Lesson
    b) The illustrations
    c) The instructions
  B. Unjust Practices (v. 4)
   1. The vulnerability of the day-laborers
   2. The default of the rich
   3. The cry of the wages
   4. The response of God

C. Self-Indulgent Spending (v. 5)
  1. Indulging in luxury
  2. Engaging in vice
  3. Pampering internal lusts
    a) A depiction of self
    b) A depiction of judgment
      (1) Previous judgment
      (2) Ultimate judgment
D. Ruthless Manipulations (v. 6*a*)
  1. The requirements for judges
  2. The corruption in the courts
III. The Beneficiaries of Judgment (v. 6*b*)

Conclusion

Introduction

A. The Character of the Wicked Rich

In the congregation to which James wrote were some who claimed to know Christ but whose lives invalidated that claim. They obviously loved money rather than God. They could have been characterized as the weedy soil of Matthew 13:22—although they initially responded to the gospel, the deceitfulness of riches choked out the Word before it could bear fruit in their lives.

B. The Character of False Teachers

A preoccupation with money is especially characteristic of false teachers. They often are engaged in the kinds of activities that bring in money. They use the name of Jesus in order to get things from people.

1. As described in 2 Peter 2

In verse 1 Peter says, "There were false prophets also among the people, even as there shall be false teachers among you . . . secretly." They are always secret—they never announce themselves to be false teachers. Matthew 7:15 calls them wolves in sheep's clothing. Since a woolen garment was the typical cloak of a prophet, false

132

teachers dressed themselves like prophets. They "bring in destructive heresies, even denying the Lord that bought them, and bring upon themselves swift destruction. And many shall follow their pernicious ways. . . . Through covetousness shall they, with feigned words, make merchandise of you" (vv. 1-3).

Verse 10 says that false teachers are presumptuous and self-willed. Peter described them as "natural brute beasts, made to be taken and destroyed" (v. 12). They "speak evil of the things that they understand not, and shall utterly perish in their own corruption, and shall receive the reward of unrighteousness, as they that count it pleasure to revel in the daytime. Spots they are and blemishes, reveling with their own deceivings while they feast with you; having eyes full of adultery and that cannot cease from sin; beguiling unstable souls; an heart they have exercised with covetous practices; cursed children, who have forsaken the right way, and are gone astray, following the way of Balaam, the son of Beor, who loved the wages of unrighteousness" (vv. 12-15). Peter also said, "When they speak great swelling words of vanity, they allure through the lusts of the flesh, through much wantonness, those that are just escaping from them who live in error. While they promise them liberty, they themselves are the servants of corruption" (vv. 18-19).

In those verses we find some facts repeated: (1) false teachers tend to be immoral, corrupt, and evil; (2) they tend to be hypocritical; and (3) they do it all for money —they make the people merchandise.

2. As described in Jude

Let's look at how Jude depicts such charlatans.

a) They teach license instead of grace—Verse 4 says, "Certain men crept in unawares . . . ungodly men, turning the grace of our God into lasciviousness." They counted on God's grace to excuse their misconduct.

b) They engage in sexual sin—Verses 7-8 say, "Even as Sodom and Gomorrah, and the cities about them in like manner, giving themselves over to fornication, and going after strange flesh. . . . In like manner also these filthy dreamers defile the flesh."

c) They defy authority—Verse 8 says they "despise dominion, and speak evil of dignities." They have no respect for the angels of God (cf. v. 9). They assert themselves to be supreme, and they believe that there is no court higher than themselves.

d) They speak evil of the things they don't understand—Verse 10 indicates that they discredit what is true and give credit to what is not.

e) They are greedy—Verse 11 says, "Woe unto them! For they have gone in the way of Cain, and ran greedily after the error of Balaam for reward."

f) They identify with true believers—Verse 12 says, "These are spots in your love feasts, when they feast with you, feeding themselves without fear; clouds they are without water, carried about by winds; trees whose fruit withereth, without fruit, twice dead, plucked up by the roots."

g) They boast about themselves—Verse 16 says, "These are murmurers, complainers, walking after their own lusts; and their mouth speaketh great swelling words."

h) They flatter others to gain an advantage—Verse 16 says, "Having men's persons in admiration because of advantage."

i) They are overwhelmed by various lusts—Verse 19 says, "These are they who separate themselves, sensual, having not the Spirit."

False teachers come with a myriad of accoutrements—it's not that difficult to discern who they are. James announces God's judgment on the wicked wealthy, whether they are ordinary people in the church or false teachers.

I. THE PRONOUNCEMENT OF JUDGMENT (v. 1; see pp. 122-23)

"Come now, ye rich men, weep and howl for your miseries that shall come upon you."

A. The Subjects of Judgment (see p. 122)

B. The Responses to Judgment

   1. Defining the response (see pp. 122-23)

   2. Calling for the response (see p. 123)

   "Weep and howl" represent inconsolable grief in light of certain doom.

   a) Isaiah 15:3-4—Isaiah said of Moab: "In their streets they shall gird themselves with sackcloth; on the tops of their houses, and in their streets, every one shall wail, weeping abundantly. And Heshbon shall cry out, and Elealeh; their voice shall be heard."

   b) Isaiah 16:7—"Therefore shall Moab wail for Moab, every one shall wail. For the foundations of Kir-hareseth shall ye mourn; surely they are stricken."

   c) Isaiah 23:1—"The burden of Tyre. Howl, ye ships of Tarshish; for it is laid waste, so that there is no house, no entering in."

   Many other Old Testament verses such as Jeremiah 48:20, Ezekiel 21:12, and Amos 8:3 call people to mourn and howl.

II. THE REASONS FOR JUDGMENT (vv. 2-6a)

A. Useless Hoarding (vv. 2-3)

1. A delineation of proper investments (see pp. 124-25)

2. A depiction of hoarding (see pp. 125-27)

3. A description of rust (see pp. 127-28)

4. A disregard for redemptive history

   a) The implications (see pp. 128-29)

Lesson

   b) The illustrations

   (1) Matthew 25:24-30—"He that had received the one talent came and said, Lord . . . I was afraid, and went and hid thy talent in the earth" (vv. 24-25). That man did nothing with the talent he was given—his lord received no return on his investment. So his lord replied, "Thou wicked and slothful servant, thou knewest that I reap where I sowed not, and gather where I have not spread. Thou oughtest, therefore, to have put my money to the exchangers, and then, at my coming, I should have received mine own with interest" (vv. 26-27). The purpose of this parable is not to promote having a good bank account or another investment vehicle. In this case investing money illustrates using what God gives you to advance His kingdom. The lord then said, "Take, therefore, the talent from him, and give it unto him who hath ten talents. For unto every one that hath shall be given, and he shall have abundance, but from him that hath not shall be taken away even that which he hath. And cast the unprofitable servant into outer darkness; there shall be weeping and gnashing of teeth" (vv. 28-30). Hell is for hoarders.

(2) 1 John 2:18—John said, "Little children, it is the last time." It is time for us to give away what we have that others might hear and believe the gospel. Our money doesn't buy salvation, but money invested to help bring people to Christ demonstrates the priority of our hearts.

(3) 1 Corinthians 7:29-31—"The time is short; it remaineth that both they that have wives be as though they had none; and they that weep, as though they wept not; and they that rejoice, as though they rejoiced not; and they that buy, as though they possessed not; and they that use this world, as not abusing it; for the fashion of this world passeth away." Paul was saying that since we're living in the end times, we're not to be preoccupied with the mundane things of life. Accept with a thankful heart either the bare essentials or the blessings from God. But take your resources and invest them in eternity, for we are living in the last days.

(4) Luke 12:19-21—The man who piles up everything he can for himself says, "Eat, drink, and be merry." But God says to him, "Thou fool, this night thy soul shall be required of thee; then whose shall those things be, which thou hast provided?" Jesus applied the lesson drawn from the example of the rich landowner: "So is he that layeth up treasure for himself, and is not rich toward God." You are a fool if you amass a fortune for yourself, thinking you can take it easy the rest of your life. Rather you should consider what God would have you do with your riches.

c) The instructions

(1) Luke 12:31-32—Jesus said, "Seek ye the kingdom of God, and all these things shall be added unto you. Fear not, little flock; for it is your Father's good pleasure to give you the kingdom." We're not going to be poor; we will be eternally rich! In verses 33-34 Jesus says, "Sell what ye have, and give alms; provide yourselves bags which grow

137

not old, a treasure in the heavens that faileth not, where no thief approacheth, neither moth corrupteth. For where your treasure is, there will your heart be also."

(2) 1 Timothy 6:17-19—"Charge them that are rich in this age, that they be not high-minded, nor trust in uncertain riches but in the living God, who giveth us richly all things to enjoy; that they do good, that they be rich in good works, ready to distribute, willing to share, laying up in store for themselves a good foundation against the time to come, that they may lay hold on eternal life." The only way to live in the light of Christ's return is to invest what God gives us in His kingdom.

B. Unjust Practices (v. 4)

"Behold, the hire of the laborers who have reaped down your fields, which is of you kept back by fraud, crieth; and the cries of them who have reaped are entered into the ears of the Lord of Sabaoth."

Instead of being generous to the poor, the wicked rich exploit them. Instead of giving the laborers the small wage that they earn, they hold it back. Verse 4 begins with "behold" because that kind of behavior is shocking and inconceivable and contrary to their claim to be Christians.

1. The vulnerability of the day-laborers

"The laborers who have reaped down your fields" is a reference to day-laborers. In the economy of Israel, the poor unskilled laborers would go to the marketplace of their village in the morning and wait, hoping that someone would come and hire them to work that day. They tended to work for whatever wage they could get since that was usually their only means of providing food for their family that day. Old Testament law was very strict regarding how an employer paid his day-laborers, and Jesus reinforced those principles.

a) Deuteronomy 24:14-15—"Thou shalt not oppress an hired servant who is poor and needy, whether he be

138

of thy brethren, or of thy sojourners who are in thy land within thy gates. At his day thou shalt give him his hire, neither shall the sun go down upon it; for he is poor, and setteth his heart upon it; lest he cry against thee unto the Lord, and it be sin unto thee."

b) Leviticus 19:13—"Thou shalt not defraud thy neighbor, neither rob him; the wages of him that is hired shall not abide with thee all night until the morning."

c) Matthew 20:1-2—"The kingdom of heaven is like a man that is an householder, who went out early in the morning to hire laborers into his vineyard. And . . . he had agreed with the laborers for a denarius a day." Throughout the day the employer hired more people, and at the end of the day chose to pay them all the same.

The hiring of day-laborers was a normal part of the economy of Israel. The agricultural cycle demanded that an employer hire extra people during the planting and harvesting seasons.

2. The default of the rich

The wicked rich "kept back by fraud" the wages due to the day-laborers (James 5:4). The Greek verb translated "kept back by fraud" (*aphustereo*) means "to withhold by default" or "to withhold by fraud." It doesn't indicate delay, which would have been bad enough. Rather it indicates total default. The wicked rich didn't pay their employees what they were due. They may have paid them something, but it wasn't the wage to which they had agreed. So the wicked rich unjustly hoarded money they gained.

3. The cry of the wages

James personified the wages that were due to the laborers, just as he personified the rust in verse 3. He said they "crieth" (Gk., *krazo*, "screaming"). That same verb describes the shrieks of demons as they tormented or went out of their victims (Mark 9:26; Luke 9:39). The wages of exploited laborers cried out to God like other inanimate objects we read about in Scripture that cry out for justice. Genesis 4:10 says the blood of Abel cried out from the ground for justice. Genesis 18:20 and 19:13 say that the sin of Sodom cried out to God.

4. The response of God

James 5:4 says, "The cries of them who have reaped are entered into the ears of the Lord of Sabaoth." It is likely that James based that statement on Deuteronomy 24:15. The painful cries of those who are victimized reach the ears of God. And they continue to echo in His righteous ears until He makes things right.

"Lord of Sabaoth" means "Lord of hosts" or "Lord of the army of heaven." Christ is the almighty commander of the hosts of heaven. The One who hears the cry of the laborers is the almighty God, who will call His army to vindicate them. Second Thessalonians 1:7-8 says, "The Lord Jesus shall be revealed from heaven with his mighty angels, in flaming fire taking vengeance on them that know not God." The angels are His agents of judgment. In the parables of judgment in Matthew 13 the angels do the reaping and the separating (vv. 41-42, 49-50). Those who have been wronged can take comfort in knowing that God will settle the matter.

C. Self-Indulgent Spending (v. 5)

"Ye have lived in pleasure on the earth, and been wanton; ye have nourished your hearts, as in a day of slaughter."

After increasing their own wealth through robbery and hoarding, the rich employers used it for their own indulgence.

1. Indulging in luxury

James said, "Ye have lived in pleasure on the earth." The Greek word translated "lived in pleasure" (*truphaō*) speaks of living in luxury or softness—easy living. They were not like Robin Hood, who stole from the rich to give to the poor. In contrast they stole from the poor to keep for themselves. God doesn't necessarily want ev-

140

eryone to sit on a box and sleep on a straw mat, but the wicked rich went beyond what was reasonable. Of John the Baptist Jesus said, "What went ye out to see? A man clothed in soft raiment? Behold, they who are gorgeously apparelled, and live delicately, are in king's courts" (Luke 7:25).

2. Engaging in vice

James 5:5 says they "led a life of wanton pleasure" (NASB). They gave themselves to vice—luxury leads to vice. Once you start living the soft life, it takes its toll. Soon you begin to be consumed with gratifying every whim. First Timothy 5:6 says, "She that liveth in pleasure is dead while she liveth." Luxurious living leads to vice and plunges people into dissipation.

Refusing to practice self-denial will probably lead you to lose control in every area. People obsessed with luxury and pleasure can't restrain themselves. They close their eyes to the needs of others and the work of God, but they open them wide to selfish pursuits.

3. Pampering internal lusts

James 5:5 then says, "Ye have nourished your hearts." The Greek word translated "nourished" (*trephō*) means "to feed" or "to fatten." It speaks of fattening up calves in Jeremiah 46:21 in the Septuagint. People who raise cattle or other animals fatten them up for slaughter. The fatter they are, the more money they bring. In like manner the wicked rich fatten their hearts by satiating their desires. They indulge themselves beyond limits. They buy whatever they want and do whatever they want. Luxurious living leads to vice, which leads to petty indulgence. When James says they fattened their "hearts," he is referring to their inner desires.

a) A depiction of self

Solomon, the author of Ecclesiastes, said the following about self-indulgence: "I made for myself great works; I built houses; I planted vineyards; I made gardens and orchards, and I planted trees in them of

141

all kind of fruits; I made pools of water, to water therewith the wood that bringeth forth trees; I got servants and maidens, and had servants born in my house; also I had great possessions of herds and flocks above all that were in Jerusalem before me. I gathered also silver and gold, and the peculiar treasure of kings and of the provinces; I got men singers and women singers, and the delights of the sons of men, as musical instruments, and that of all sorts. So I was great, and increased more than all that were before me in Jerusalem, also my wisdom remained with me. And whatsoever mine eyes desired, I kept not from them. I withheld not my heart from any joy; for my heart rejoiced in all my labor; and this was my portion of all my labor. Then I looked on all the works that my hands had wrought, and on the labor that I had labored to do; and, behold, all was vanity and vexation of spirit, and there was no profit under the sun" (Eccles. 2:4-11). Worse than yielding no profit, which could be thought of as a neutral result, self-indulgence brings about a negative result—God's judgment.

b) A depiction of judgment

"A day of slaughter" (James 5:5) is a frightening depiction of judgment. In those days they slaughtered animals by slitting their throats. The wicked rich were just like a herd of fattened cattle headed to the slaughterhouse to have their throats slit. Their only hope for a reprieve was to repent of their sin and embrace true saving faith.

(1) Previous judgment

(a) Isaiah 34:5-8—"My sword shall be bathed in heaven; behold, it shall come down upon Edom, and upon the people of my curse, to judgment. The sword of the Lord is filled with blood; it is made fat with fatness, and with the blood of lambs and goats, with the fat of the kidneys of rams; for the Lord hath a sacrifice in Bozrah, and a great slaughter in the land of Edom. And the wild oxen shall come down

142

with them, and the bullocks with the bulls; and their land shall be soaked with blood, and their dust made fat with fatness. For it is the day of the Lord's vengeance." That is a good indication of what James had in mind when he said "a day of slaughter." He was referring to a day of vengeance—the day of judgment of the wicked.

(b) Jeremiah 46:10—"This is the day of the Lord God of hosts, a day of vengeance, that he may avenge himself on his adversaries; and the sword shall devour, and it shall be filled to the full and made drunk with their blood."

(c) Jeremiah 50:26—"Come against her from the utmost border, open her storehouses; cast her up as heaps, and destroy her utterly; let nothing of her be left. Slay all her bullocks; let them go down to the slaughter. Woe unto them! For their day is come, the time of their judgment."

There were many days of the Lord. Whenever God came in judgment it was considered a day of the Lord. There are days of the Lord for wicked rich people of every age.

(2) Ultimate judgment

James looks ahead to a day yet to come when Christ and the holy angels come in flaming fire to take vengeance on those who don't know God and have rejected Jesus Christ (2 Thess. 1:7-8). Revelation 19:17-18 says, "I saw an angel standing in the sun; and he cried with a loud voice, saying to all the fowls that fly in the midst of heaven, Come and gather yourselves together unto the supper of the great God, that ye may eat the flesh of kings, and the flesh of captains, and the flesh of mighty men, and the flesh of horses and of them that sit on them, and the flesh of all men, both free and enslaved, both small and great." That's the slaughter that will take place at

143

the Battle of Armageddon. The coming of Christ will bring it about. Verse 11 says He will charge on a white horse, and verse 15 says, "Out of his mouth goeth a sharp sword, that with it he should smite the nations."

There are many days of the Lord in which God brings vengeance and judgment. When a wicked wealthy person dies, he faces God in judgment. In a sense that is the day of the Lord for him. But a final judgment is coming, which will result in slaughter.

D. Ruthless Manipulations (v. 6a)

"Ye have condemned and killed the just."

Hoarding led to fraud, which led to self-indulgence. At that point some will do anything to sustain their life-style —including murder. James implies that such men use the courts to condemn innocent people.

1. The requirements for judges

In the Old Testament God established courts in Israel where justice could be carried out (Deut. 17:8-13). He commanded the judges not to be greedy (Ex. 18:21) or to show favoritism (Lev. 19:15). They were not to tolerate perjury (Deut. 19:16-21) or bribery (Isa. 33:15; Mic. 3:11; 7:3). They were to seek justice for everyone.

2. The corruption in the courts

However, even in Israel there was tremendous corruption. Amos 5:12 says, "I know your manifold transgressions and your mighty sins; they afflict the just, they take a bribe, and they turn aside the poor in the gate." Verse 15 says, "Hate the evil, and love the good, and establish justice." The leaders had perjured themselves, taken bribes, and perverted justice.

The Greek word translated "condemn" (katadikazō) means "to sentence someone." The Greek word translated "put to death" (phoneuō) means "to murder." The wicked rich sentenced people and in effect murdered

144

them. They used the courts to deal with people who got in their way. James 2:6 alludes to that: "Ye have despised the poor. Do not rich men oppress you, and draw you before the judgment seats?" That portrays what people had to endure at the hands of greedy rich people. Today people continue to use the courts to grow rich and abuse the innocent.

III. THE BENEFICIARIES OF JUDGMENT (v. 6b)

"He doth not resist you."

It is difficult to be dogmatic about who "he" represents. But it seems best to assume he is the innocent party being abused by the rich. Perhaps he's a believer who won't fight back because he wants to be like his Lord, of whom Peter said, "When he was reviled, [he] reviled not again; when he suffered, he threatened not, but committed himself to him that judgeth righteously" (1 Pet. 2:23). Perhaps he wants to live out this truth from the Sermon on the Mount: "Whosoever shall smite thee on thy right cheek, turn to him the other also. And if any man will sue thee at the law, and take away thy coat, let him have thy cloak also. And whosoever shall compel thee to go a mile, go with him two. Give to him that asketh thee, and from him that would borrow of thee turn not thou away" (Matt. 5:39-42). The Greek word translated "just" in James 5:5 means "righteous." The one who doesn't resist is righteous—he doesn't fight back. Perhaps he's so rich in faith that he commits himself to God as Christ did.

Conclusion

Why are the wicked rich condemned? Because of their useless hoarding, unjust practices, self-indulgent spending, and ruthless manipulations. They fulfill their lusts at the expense of anyone who gets in their way. It is sinful to waste the riches with which God has blessed us.

Count Zinzendorf lived from 1700 to 1760. He was instrumental in beginning the missionary society known as the Moravian Brethren, a pioneer group in world missions. The Count was very wealthy, but he gave everything he had to the ministry for the spreading of

145

the gospel. That kind of life is the antithesis of everything we see described in James 5:1-6. Anyone with extra resources makes a choice either to use them for the kingdom or waste them and receive the judgment of God.

James wrote that passage to those who claimed to be Christians but were not, as evidenced by their love of money. Yet as believers we can learn from it, too. We don't want to imitate the sins of hypocrites. We must be sure to use what God has given us to advance his kingdom and to glorify the Lord. And we must be sure that we don't love the things of the world. We must use whatever assets we have to exalt Christ, especially in these last days.

Focusing on the Facts

1. What group of people characteristically loves money (see p. 132)?
2. How are those people described in 2 Peter and Jude (see pp. 132-34)?
3. What does Matthew 25:24-30 teach about those who hoard their money (see p. 136)?
4. Instead of being generous to the poor, how did the wicked rich treat them (James 5:4; see p. 138)?
5. What provisions did God make for day-laborers in the Old Testament (see pp. 138-39)?
6. In what way did the wicked rich defraud the day-laborers (see p. 139)?
7. In what way does the title "Lord of Sabaoth" relate to the coming judgment (see p. 140)?
8. In what ways did the wicked rich indulge themselves? Be specific (see pp. 140-41).
9. In what way are the wicked rich like fattened calves (see p. 141)?
10. What was Solomon's conclusion about self-indulgence (Eccles. 2:4-11; see pp. 141-42)?
11. What does "a day of slaughter" depict (see p. 142)?
12. To what particular day was James referring (see p. 143)?
13. What will the wicked rich often do in order to sustain their lifestyle (James 5:6; see p. 144)?
14. To whom might the "he" in James 5:6 refer (see p. 145)?

Pondering the Principles

1. What is your attitude toward the poor in your community? Look up the following verses: Psalm 41:1-3; Proverbs 28:27; Mark 14:7; Luke 14:12-14; 1 John 3:17-19. What do those verses teach about your duty to the poor? What happens to those who help the poor? Have you had opportunities to give to the poor? How did you feel when you were able to give something? How did you feel when you didn't because you didn't have the time or didn't want to let go of certain things? Read Matthew 25:34-40. When you give to the poor, remember to Whom you're also giving. Let that motivate you to sacrifice some of the abundance God has given you to support those in need.

2. In this study of James 5:1-6 we have concentrated on the wicked rich but not on their victims. Many of us can't relate to wicked rich people, but we can relate to those who have been victimized by them. How would you respond if your employer didn't pay what he owed you? How would you respond if a wealthy individual used the court system to steal from you and put you in jail? Read 1 Peter 2:23. Why was Christ able to endure as He did without retaliating? Whenever you're faced with injustice, make that same commitment to entrust yourself to Him who judges righteously.

Scripture Index

151

153

Topical Index